The
Woman
Warrior

The

Woman

Warrior

MEMOIRS OF
A GIRLHOOD
AMONG GHOSTS

Maxine

Hong

Kingston

VINTAGE INTERNATIONAL

VINTAGE BOOKS

A DIVISION OF RANDOM HOUSE, INC.

NEW YORK

Vintage International Edition, April 1989

Library of Congress Cataloging in Publication Data
Kingston, Maxine Hong.
The woman warrior.
1.   Kingston, Maxine Hong.   2.   United States—
Biography.   I.   Title.
[CT275.K5764A33   1977]   979.4'61'050924
[B]   77-3246
ISBN 679-72188-6 (pbk.)

"No Name Woman" originally appeared, in slightly
different form, in the January 1975 issue of *Viva*.

Manufactured in the United States of America
D987654

To Mother and Father

Contents

No

Name

Woman

"You must not tell anyone," my mother said, "what I am about to tell you. In China your father had a sister who killed herself. She jumped into the family well. We say that your father has all brothers because it is as if she had never been born.

"In 1924 just a few days after our village celebrated seventeen hurry-up weddings—to make sure that every young man who went 'out on the road' would responsibly come home—your father and his brothers and your grandfather and his brothers and your aunt's new husband sailed for America, the Gold Mountain. It was your grandfather's last trip. Those lucky enough to get contracts waved goodbye from the decks. They fed and guarded the stowaways and helped them off in Cuba, New York, Bali, Hawaii. 'We'll meet in California next year,' they said. All of them sent money home.

"I remember looking at your aunt one day when she and I were dressing; I had not noticed before that she had such a protruding melon of a stomach. But I did not think, 'She's pregnant,' until she began to look like other pregnant women, her shirt pulling and the white tops of her black pants showing. She could not have been pregnant, you see, because her husband had been gone for years. No one said anything. We did not discuss it. In early summer she was ready to have the child, long after the time when it could have been possible.

"The village had also been counting. On the night the baby was to be born the villagers raided our house. Some were crying. Like a great saw, teeth strung with lights, files of people walked zigzag across our land, tearing the rice. Their lanterns doubled in the disturbed black water, which drained away through the broken bunds. As the villagers closed in, we could see that some of them, probably men and women we knew well, wore white masks. The people with long hair hung it over their faces. Women with short hair made it stand up on end. Some had tied white bands around their foreheads, arms, and legs.

"At first they threw mud and rocks at the house. Then they threw eggs and began slaughtering our stock. We could hear the animals scream their deaths—the roosters, the pigs, a last great roar from the ox. Familiar wild heads flared in our night windows; the villagers encircled us. Some of the faces stopped to peer at us, their eyes rushing like searchlights. The hands flattened against the panes, framed heads, and left red prints.

"The villagers broke in the front and the back doors at the same time, even though we had not locked the doors against them. Their knives dripped with the blood of our animals. They smeared blood on the doors and walls. One woman swung a chicken, whose throat she had slit, splattering blood in red arcs about her. We stood together in the middle of our house, in the family hall with the pictures and tables of the ancestors around us, and looked straight ahead.

"At that time the house had only two wings. When the men came back, we would build two more to enclose our courtyard and a third one to begin a second courtyard. The villagers pushed through both wings, even your grandparents' rooms, to find your aunt's, which was also mine until the men returned. From this room a new wing for one of the younger families would grow. They ripped up her clothes and shoes and broke her combs, grinding them underfoot. They tore her work from the loom. They scattered the cooking fire and rolled the new weaving in it. We could hear them in the kitchen breaking our bowls and banging the pots. They overturned the great waist-high earthenware jugs; duck eggs, pickled fruits, vegetables burst out and mixed in acrid torrents. The old woman from the next field swept a broom through the air and loosed the spirits-of-the-broom over our heads. 'Pig.' 'Ghost.' 'Pig,' they sobbed and scolded while they ruined our house.

"When they left, they took sugar and oranges to bless themselves. They cut pieces from the dead animals. Some of them took bowls that were not broken and clothes that were not torn. Afterward we swept up the rice and sewed it back up into sacks. But the smells from the spilled preserves lasted. Your aunt gave birth in the pigsty that night. The next morning when I went for the water, I found her and the baby plugging up the family well.

"Don't let your father know that I told you. He denies her. Now that you have started to menstruate, what happened to her could happen to you. Don't humiliate us. You wouldn't like to be forgotten as if you had never been born. The villagers are watchful."

Whenever she had to warn us about life, my mother told stories that ran like this one, a story to grow up on. She tested our strength to establish realities. Those in the emigrant generations who could not reassert brute survival died young and far from home. Those of us in the first American generations have had to figure out how the invisible world the emigrants built around our childhoods fits in solid America.

The emigrants confused the gods by diverting their curses, misleading them with crooked streets and false names. They must try to confuse their offspring as well, who, I suppose, threaten them in similar ways—always trying to get things straight, always trying to name the unspeakable. The Chinese I know hide their names; sojourners take new names when their lives change and guard their real names with silence.

Chinese-Americans, when you try to understand what things in you are Chinese, how do you separate what is peculiar to childhood, to poverty, insanities, one family, your mother who marked your growing with stories, from what is Chinese? What is Chinese tradition and what is the movies?

If I want to learn what clothes my aunt wore, whether flashy or ordinary, I would have to begin, "Remember Father's drowned-in-the-well sister?" I cannot ask that. My mother has told me once and for all the useful parts. She will add nothing unless powered by Necessity, a riverbank that guides her life. She plants vegetable gardens rather than lawns; she carries the odd-shaped tomatoes home from the fields and eats food left for the gods.

Whenever we did frivolous things, we used up energy; we flew high kites. We children came up off the ground over the melting cones our parents brought home from work and the American movie on New Year's Day—*Oh, You Beautiful Doll* with Betty Grable one year, and *She Wore a Yellow Ribbon* with John Wayne another year. After the one carnival ride each, we paid in guilt; our tired father counted his change on the dark walk home.

Adultery is extravagance. Could people who hatch their own chicks and eat the embryos and the heads for delicacies and boil the feet in vinegar for party food, leaving only the gravel, eating even the gizzard lining—could such people engender a prodigal aunt? To be a woman, to have a daughter in starvation time was a waste enough. My aunt could not have been the lone romantic who gave up everything for sex. Women in the old China did not choose. Some man had commanded her to lie with him and be his secret evil. I wonder whether he masked himself when he joined the raid on her family.

Perhaps she had encountered him in the fields or on the mountain where the daughters-in-law collected fuel. Or perhaps he first noticed her in the marketplace. He was not a stranger because the village housed no strangers. She had to have dealings with him other than sex. Perhaps he worked an adjoining field, or he sold her the cloth for the dress she sewed and wore. His demand must have surprised, then terrified her. She obeyed him; she always did as she was told.

When the family found a young man in the next village to be her husband, she had stood tractably beside the best rooster, his proxy, and promised before they met that she would be his forever. She was lucky that he was her age and she would be the first wife, an advantage secure now. The night she first saw him, he had sex with her. Then he left for America. She had almost forgotten what he looked like. When she tried to envision him, she only saw the black and white face in the group photograph the men had had taken before leaving.

The other man was not, after all, much different from her husband. They both gave orders: she followed. "If you tell your family, I'll beat you. I'll kill you. Be here again next week." No one talked sex, ever. And she might have separated the rapes from the rest of living if only she did not have to buy her oil from him or gather wood in the same forest. I want her fear to have lasted just as long as rape lasted so that the fear could have been contained. No drawn-out fear. But women at sex hazarded birth and hence lifetimes. The fear did not stop but permeated everywhere. She told the man, "I think I'm pregnant." He organized the raid against her.

On nights when my mother and father talked about their life back home, sometimes they mentioned an "outcast table" whose business they still seemed to be settling, their voices tight. In a commensal tradition, where food is precious, the powerful older people made wrongdoers eat alone. Instead of letting them start separate new lives like the Japanese, who could become samurais and geishas, the Chinese family, faces averted but eyes glowering sideways, hung on to the offenders and fed them leftovers. My aunt must have lived in the same house as my parents and eaten at an outcast table. My mother spoke about the raid as if she had seen it, when she and my aunt, a daughter-in-law to a different household, should not have been living together at all. Daughters-in-law lived with their husbands' parents, not their own; a synonym for marriage in Chinese is "taking a daughter-in-law." Her husband's parents could have sold her, mortgaged her, stoned her. But they had sent her back to her own mother and father, a mysterious act hinting at disgraces not told me. Perhaps they had thrown her out to deflect the avengers.

She was the only daughter; her four brothers went with her father, husband, and uncles "out on the road" and for some years became western men. When the goods were divided among the family, three of the brothers took land, and the youngest, my father, chose an education. After my grandparents gave their daughter away to her husband's family, they had dispensed all the adventure and all the property. They expected her alone to keep the traditional ways, which her brothers, now among the barbarians, could fumble without detection. The heavy, deep-rooted women were to maintain the past against the flood, safe for returning. But the rare urge west had fixed upon our family, and so my aunt crossed boundaries not delineated in space.

The work of preservation demands that the feelings playing about in one's guts not be turned into action. Just watch their passing like cherry blossoms. But perhaps my aunt, my forerunner, caught in a slow life, let dreams grow and fade and after some months or years went toward what persisted. Fear at the enormities of the forbidden kept her desires delicate, wire and bone. She looked at a man because she liked the way the hair was tucked behind his ears, or she liked the question-mark line of a long torso curving at the shoulder and straight at the hip. For warm eyes or a soft voice or a slow walk—that's all—a few hairs, a line, a brightness, a sound, a pace, she gave up family. She offered us up for a charm that vanished with tiredness, a pigtail that didn't toss when the wind died. Why, the wrong lighting could erase the dearest thing about him.

It could very well have been, however, that my aunt did not take subtle enjoyment of her friend, but, a wild woman, kept rollicking company. Imagining her free with sex doesn't fit, though. I don't know any women like that, or men either. Unless I see her life branching into mine, she gives me no ancestral help.

To sustain her being in love, she often worked at herself in the mirror, guessing at the colors and shapes that would interest him, changing them frequently in order to hit on the right combination. She wanted him to look back.

On a farm near the sea, a woman who tended her appearance reaped a reputation for eccentricity. All the married women blunt-cut their hair in flaps about their ears or pulled it back in tight buns. No nonsense. Neither style blew easily into heart-catching tangles. And at their weddings they displayed themselves in their long hair for the last time. "It brushed the backs of my knees," my mother tells me. "It was braided, and even so, it brushed the backs of my knees."

At the mirror my aunt combed individuality into her bob. A bun could have been contrived to escape into black streamers blowing in the wind or in quiet wisps about her face, but only the older women in our picture album wear buns. She brushed her hair back from her forehead, tucking the flaps behind her ears. She looped a piece of thread, knotted into a circle between her index fingers and thumbs, and ran the double strand across her forehead. When she closed her fingers as if she were making a pair of shadow geese bite, the string twisted together catching the little hairs. Then she pulled the thread away from her skin, ripping the hairs out neatly, her eyes watering from the needles of pain. Opening her fingers, she cleaned the thread, then rolled it along her hairline and the tops of her eyebrows. My mother did the same to me and my sisters and herself. I used to believe that the expression "caught by the short hairs" meant a captive held with a depilatory string. It especially hurt at the temples, but my mother said we were lucky we didn't have to have our feet bound when we were seven. Sisters used to sit on their beds and cry together, she said, as their mothers or their slaves removed the bandages for a few minutes each night and let the blood gush back into their veins. I hope that the man my aunt loved appreciated a smooth brow, that he wasn't just a tits-and-ass man.

Once my aunt found a freckle on her chin, at a spot that the almanac said predestined her for unhappiness. She dug it out with a hot needle and washed the wound with peroxide.

More attention to her looks than these pullings of hairs and pickings at spots would have caused gossip among the villagers. They owned work clothes and good clothes, and they wore good clothes for feasting the new seasons. But since a woman combing her hair hexes beginnings, my aunt rarely found an occasion to look her best. Women looked like great sea snails—the corded wood, babies, and laundry they carried were the whorls on their backs. The Chinese did not admire a bent back; goddesses and warriors stood straight. Still there must have been a marvelous freeing of beauty when a worker laid down her burden and stretched and arched.

Such commonplace loveliness, however, was not enough for my aunt. She dreamed of a lover for the fifteen days of New Year's, the time for families to exchange visits, money, and food. She plied her secret comb. And sure enough she cursed the year, the family, the village, and herself.

Even as her hair lured her imminent lover, many other men looked at her. Uncles, cousins, nephews, brothers would have looked, too, had they been home between journeys. Perhaps they had already been restraining their curiosity, and they left, fearful that their glances, like a field of nesting birds, might be startled and caught. Poverty hurt, and that was their first reason for leaving. But another, final reason for leaving the crowded house was the never-said.

She may have been unusually beloved, the precious only daughter, spoiled and mirror gazing because of the affection the family lavished on her. When her husband left, they welcomed the chance to take her back from the in-laws; she could live like the little daughter for just a while longer. There are stories that my grandfather was different from other people, "crazy ever since the little Jap bayoneted him in the head." He used to put his naked penis on the dinner table, laughing. And one day he brought home a baby girl, wrapped up inside his brown western-style greatcoat. He had traded one of his sons, probably my father, the youngest, for her. My grandmother made him trade back. When he finally got a daughter of his own, he doted on her. They must have all loved her, except perhaps my father, the only brother who never went back to China, having once been traded for a girl.

Brothers and sisters, newly men and women, had to efface their sexual color and present plain miens. Disturbing hair and eyes, a smile like no other, threatened the ideal of five generations living under one roof. To focus blurs, people shouted face to face and yelled from room to room. The immigrants I know have loud voices, unmodulated to American tones even after years away from the village where they called their friendships out across the fields. I have not been able to stop my mother's screams in public libraries or over telephones. Walking erect (knees straight, toes pointed forward, not pigeon-toed, which is Chinese-feminine) and speaking in an inaudible voice, I have tried to turn myself American-feminine. Chinese communication was loud, public. Only sick people had to whisper. But at the dinner table, where the family members came nearest one another, no one could talk, not the outcasts nor any eaters. Every word that falls from the mouth is a coin lost. Silently they gave and accepted food with both hands. A preoccupied child who took his bowl with one hand got a sideways glare. A complete moment of total attention is due everyone alike. Children and lovers have no singularity here, but my aunt used a secret voice, a separate attentiveness.

She kept the man's name to herself throughout her labor and dying; she did not accuse him that he be punished with her. To save her inseminator's name she gave silent birth.

He may have been somebody in her own household, but intercourse with a man outside the family would have been no less abhorrent. All the village were kinsmen, and the titles shouted in loud country voices never let kinship be forgotten. Any man within visiting distance would have been neutralized as a lover—"brother," "younger brother," "older brother"—one hundred and fifteen relationship titles. Parents researched birth charts probably not so much to assure good fortune as to circumvent incest in a population that has but one hundred surnames. Everybody has eight million relatives. How useless then sexual mannerisms, how dangerous.

As if it came from an atavism deeper than fear, I used to add "brother" silently to boys' names. It hexed the boys, who would or would not ask me to dance, and made them less scary and as familiar and deserving of benevolence as girls.

But, of course, I hexed myself also—no dates. I should have stood up, both arms waving, and shouted out across libraries, "Hey, you! Love me back." I had no idea, though, how to make attraction selective, how to control its direction and magnitude. If I made myself American-pretty so that the five or six Chinese boys in the class fell in love with me, everyone else—the Caucasian, Negro, and Japanese boys—would too. Sisterliness, dignified and honorable, made much more sense.

Attraction eludes control so stubbornly that whole societies designed to organize relationships among people cannot keep order, not even when they bind people to one another from childhood and raise them together. Among the very poor and the wealthy, brothers married their adopted sisters, like doves. Our family allowed some romance, paying adult brides' prices and providing dowries so that their sons and daughters could marry strangers. Marriage promises to turn strangers into friendly relatives—a nation of siblings.

In the village structure, spirits shimmered among the live creatures, balanced and held in equilibrium by time and land. But one human being flaring up into violence could open up a black hole, a maelstrom that pulled in the sky. The frightened villagers, who depended on one another to maintain the real, went to my aunt to show her a personal, physical representation of the break she had made in the "roundness." Misallying couples snapped off the future, which was to be embodied in true offspring. The villagers punished her for acting as if she could have a private life, secret and apart from them.

If my aunt had betrayed the family at a time of large grain yields and peace, when many boys were born, and wings were being built on many houses, perhaps she might have escaped such severe punishment. But the men—hungry, greedy, tired of planting in dry soil—had been forced to leave the village in order to send food-money home. There were ghost plagues, bandit plagues, wars with the Japanese, floods. My Chinese brother and sister had died of an unknown sickness. Adultery, perhaps only a mistake during good times, became a crime when the village needed food.

The round moon cakes and round doorways, the round tables of graduated sizes that fit one roundness inside another, round windows and rice bowls—these talismans had lost their power to warn this family of the law: a family must be whole, faithfully keeping the descent line by having sons to feed the old and the dead, who in turn look after the family. The villagers came to show my aunt and her lover-in-hiding a broken house. The villagers were speeding up the circling of events because she was too shortsighted to see that her infidelity had already harmed the village, that waves of consequences would return unpredictably, sometimes in disguise, as now, to hurt her. This roundness had to be made coin-sized so that she would see its circumference: punish her at the birth of her baby. Awaken her to the inexorable. People who refused fatalism because they could invent small resources insisted on culpability. Deny accidents and wrest fault from the stars.

After the villagers left, their lanterns now scattering in various directions toward home, the family broke their silence and cursed her. "Aiaa, we're going to die. Death is coming. Death is coming. Look what you've done. You've killed us. Ghost! Dead ghost! Ghost! You've never been born." She ran out into the fields, far enough from the house so that she could no longer hear their voices, and pressed herself against the earth, her own land no more. When she felt the birth coming, she thought that she had been hurt. Her body seized together. "They've hurt me too much," she thought. "This is gall, and it will kill me." With forehead and knees against the earth, her body convulsed and then relaxed. She turned on her back, lay on the ground. The black well of sky and stars went out and out and out forever; her body and her complexity seemed to disappear. She was one of the stars, a bright dot in blackness, without home, without a companion, in eternal cold and silence. An agoraphobia rose in her, speeding higher and higher, bigger and bigger; she would not be able to contain it; there would no end to fear.

Flayed, unprotected against space, she felt pain return, focusing her body. This pain chilled her—a cold, steady kind of surface pain. Inside, spasmodically, the other pain, the pain of the child, heated her. For hours she lay on the ground, alternately body and space. Sometimes a vision of normal comfort obliterated reality: she saw the family in the evening gambling at the dinner table, the young people massaging their elders' backs. She saw them congratulating one another, high joy on the mornings the rice shoots came up. When these pictures burst, the stars drew yet further apart. Black space opened.

She got to her feet to fight better and remembered that old-fashioned women gave birth in their pigsties to fool the jealous, pain-dealing gods, who do not snatch piglets. Before the next spasms could stop her, she ran to the pigsty, each step a rushing out into emptiness. She climbed over the fence and knelt in the dirt. It was good to have a fence enclosing her, a tribal person alone.

Laboring, this woman who had carried her child as a foreign growth that sickened her every day, expelled it at last. She reached down to touch the hot, wet, moving mass, surely smaller than anything human, and could feel that it was human after all—fingers, toes, nails, nose. She pulled it up on to her belly, and it lay curled there, butt in the air, feet precisely tucked one under the other. She opened her loose shirt and buttoned the child inside. After resting, it squirmed and thrashed and she pushed it up to her breast. It turned its head this way and that until it found her nipple. There, it made little snuffling noises. She clenched her teeth at its preciousness, lovely as a young calf, a piglet, a little dog.

She may have gone to the pigsty as a last act of responsibility: she would protect this child as she had protected its father. It would look after her soul, leaving supplies on her grave. But how would this tiny child without family find her grave when there would be no marker for her anywhere, neither in the earth nor the family hall? No one would give her a family hall name. She had taken the child with her into the wastes. At its birth the two of them had felt the same raw pain of separation, a wound that only the family pressing tight could close. A child with no descent line would not soften her life but only trail after her, ghostlike, begging her to give it purpose. At dawn the villagers on their way to the fields would stand around the fence and look.

Full of milk, the little ghost slept. When it awoke, she hardened her breasts against the milk that crying loosens. Toward morning she picked up the baby and walked to the well.

Carrying the baby to the well shows loving. Otherwise abandon it. Turn its face into the mud. Mothers who love their children take them along. It was probably a girl; there is some hope of forgiveness for boys.

"Don't tell anyone you had an aunt. Your father does not want to hear her name. She has never been born." I have believed that sex was unspeakable and words so strong and fathers so frail that "aunt" would do my father mysterious harm. I have thought that my family, having settled among immigrants who had also been their neighbors in the ancestral land, needed to clean their name, and a wrong word would incite the kinspeople even here. But there is more to this silence: they want me to participate in her punishment. And I have.

In the twenty years since I heard this story I have not asked for details nor said my aunt's name; I do not know it. People who can comfort the dead can also chase after them to hurt them further—a reverse ancestor worship. The real punishment was not the raid swiftly inflicted by the villagers, but the family's deliberately forgetting her. Her betrayal so maddened them, they saw to it that she would suffer forever, even after death. Always hungry, always needing, she would have to beg food from other ghosts, snatch and steal it from those whose living descendants give them gifts. She would have to fight the ghosts massed at crossroads for the buns a few thoughtful citizens leave to decoy her away from village and home so that the ancestral spirits could feast unharassed. At peace, they could act like gods, not ghosts, their descent lines providing them with paper suits and dresses, spirit money, paper houses, paper automobiles, chicken, meat, and rice into eternity— essences delivered up in smoke and flames, steam and incense rising from each rice bowl. In an attempt to make the Chinese care for people outside the family, Chairman Mao encourages us now to give our paper replicas to the spirits of outstanding soldiers and workers, no matter whose ancestors they may be. My aunt remains forever hungry. Goods are not distributed evenly among the dead.

My aunt haunts me—her ghost drawn to me because now, after fifty years of neglect, I alone devote pages of paper to her, though not origamied into houses and clothes. I do not think she always means me well. I am telling on her, and she was a spite suicide, drowning herself in the drinking water. The Chinese are always very frightened of the drowned one, whose weeping ghost, wet hair hanging and skin bloated, waits silently by the water to pull down a substitute.

White

Tigers

When we Chinese girls listened to the adults talk-story, we learned that we failed if we grew up to be but wives or slaves. We could be heroines, swordswomen. Even if she had to rage across all China, a swordswoman got even with anybody who hurt her family. Perhaps women were once so dangerous that they had to have their feet bound. It was a woman who invented white crane boxing only two hundred years ago. She was already an expert pole fighter, daughter of a teacher trained at the Shao-lin temple, where there lived an order of fighting monks. She was combing her hair one morning when a white crane alighted outside her window. She teased it with her pole, which it pushed aside with a soft brush of its wing. Amazed, she dashed outside and tried to knock the crane off its perch. It snapped her pole in two. Recognizing the presence of great power, she asked the spirit of the white crane if it would teach her to fight. It answered with a cry that white crane boxers imitate today. Later the bird returned as an old man, and he guided her boxing for many years. Thus she gave the world a new martial art.

This was one of the tamer, more modern stories, mere introduction. My mother told others that followed swordswomen through woods and palaces for years. Night after night my mother would talk-story until we fell asleep. I couldn't tell where the stories left off and the dreams began, her voice the voice of the heroines in my sleep. And on Sundays, from noon to midnight, we went to the movies at the Confucius Church. We saw swordswomen jump over houses from a standstill; they didn't even need a running start.

At last I saw that I too had been in the presence of

great power, my mother talking-story. After I grew up, I heard the chant of Fa Mu Lan, the girl who took her father's place in battle. Instantly I remembered that as a child I had followed my mother about the house, the two of us singing about how Fa Mu Lan fought gloriously and returned alive from war to settle in the village. I had forgotten this chant that was once mine, given me by my mother, who may not have known its power to remind. She said I would grow up a wife and a slave, but she taught me the song of the warrior woman, Fa Mu Lan. I would have to grow up a warrior woman.

The call would come from a bird that flew over our roof. In the brush drawings it looks like the ideograph for "human," two black wings. The bird would cross the sun and lift into the mountains (which look like the ideograph "mountain"), there parting the mist briefly that swirled opaque again. I would be a little girl of seven the day I followed the bird away into the mountains. The brambles would tear off my shoes and the rocks cut my feet and fingers, but I would keep climbing, eyes upward to follow the bird. We would go around and around the tallest mountain, climbing ever upward. I would drink from the river, which I would meet again and again. We would go so high the plants would change, and the river that flows past the village would become a waterfall. At the height where the bird used to disappear, the clouds would gray the world like an ink wash.

Even when I got used to that gray, I would only see peaks as if shaded in pencil, rocks like charcoal rubbings, everything so murky. There would be just two black strokes —the bird. Inside the clouds—inside the dragon's breath— I would not know how many hours or days passed. Suddenly, without noise, I would break clear into a yellow, warm world. New trees would lean toward me at mountain angles, but when I looked for the village, it would have vanished under the clouds.

The bird, now gold so close to the sun, would come to

rest on the thatch of a hut, which, until the bird's two feet touched it, was camouflaged as part of the mountainside.

The door opened, and an old man and an old woman came out carrying bowls of rice and soup and a leafy branch of peaches.

"Have you eaten rice today, little girl?" they greeted me.

"Yes, I have," I said out of politeness. "Thank you."

("No, I haven't," I would have said in real life, mad at the Chinese for lying so much. "I'm starved. Do you have any cookies? I like chocolate chip cookies.")

"We were about to sit down to another meal," the old woman said. "Why don't you eat with us?"

They just happened to be bringing three rice bowls and three pairs of silver chopsticks out to the plank table under the pines. They gave me an egg, as if it were my birthday, and tea, though they were older than I, but I poured for them. The teapot and the rice pot seemed bottomless, but perhaps not; the old couple ate very little except for peaches.

When the mountains and the pines turned into blue oxen, blue dogs, and blue people standing, the old couple asked me to spend the night in the hut. I thought about the long way down in the ghostly dark and decided yes. The inside of the hut seemed as large as the outdoors. Pine needles covered the floor in thick patterns; someone had carefully arranged the yellow, green, and brown pine needles according to age. When I stepped carelessly and mussed a line, my feet kicked up new blends of earth colors, but the old man and old woman walked so lightly that their feet never stirred the designs by a needle.

A rock grew in the middle of the house, and that was their table. The benches were fallen trees. Ferns and shade flowers grew out of one wall, the mountainside itself. The old couple tucked me into a bed just my width. "Breathe evenly, or you'll lose your balance and fall out," said the woman, covering me with a silk bag stuffed with feathers and herbs. "Opera singers, who begin their training at age five, sleep in beds like this." Then the two of them went outside, and through the window I could see them pull on a rope looped over a branch. The rope was tied to the roof, and the roof opened up like a basket lid. I would sleep with the moon and the stars. I did not see whether the old people slept, so quickly did I drop off, but they would be there waking me with food in the morning.

"Little girl, you have now spent almost a day and a night with us," the old woman said. In the morning light I could see her earlobes pierced with gold. "Do you think you can bear to stay with us for fifteen years? We can train you to become a warrior."

"What about my mother and father?" I asked.

The old man untied the drinking gourd slung across his back. He lifted the lid by its stem and looked for something in the water. "Ah, there," he said.

At first I saw only water so clear it magnified the fibers in the walls of the gourd. On the surface, I saw only my own round reflection. The old man encircled the neck of the gourd with his thumb and index finger and gave it a shake. As the water shook, then settled, the colors and lights shimmered into a picture, not reflecting anything I could see around me. There at the bottom of the gourd were my mother and father scanning the sky, which was where I was. "It has happened already, then," I could hear my mother say. "I didn't expect it so soon." "You knew from her birth that she would be taken," my father answered. "We'll have to harvest potatoes without her help this year," my mother said, and they turned away toward the fields, straw baskets in their arms. The water shook and became just water again. "Mama. Papa," I called, but they were in the valley and could not hear me.

"What do you want to do?" the old man asked. "You can go back right now if you like. You can go pull sweet potatoes, or you can stay with us and learn how to fight barbarians and bandits."

"You can avenge your village," said the old woman. "You can recapture the harvests the thieves have taken. You can be remembered by the Han people for your dutifulness."

"I'll stay with you," I said.

So the hut became my home, and I found out that the old woman did not arrange the pine needles by hand. She opened the roof; an autumn wind would come up, and the needles fell in braids—brown strands, green strands, yellow strands. The old woman waved her arms in conducting motions; she blew softly with her mouth. I thought, nature certainly works differently on mountains than in valleys.

"The first thing you have to learn," the old woman told me, "is how to be quiet." They left me by streams to watch for animals. "If you're noisy, you'll make the deer go without water."

When I could kneel all day without my legs cramping and my breathing became even, the squirrels would bury their hoardings at the hem of my shirt and then bend their tails in a celebration dance. At night, the mice and toads looked at me, their eyes quick stars and slow stars. Not once would I see a three-legged toad, though; you need strings of cash to bait them.

The two old people led me in exercises that began at dawn and ended at sunset so that I could watch our shadows grow and shrink and grow again, rooted to the earth. I learned to move my fingers, hands, feet, head, and entire body in circles. I walked putting heel down first, toes pointing outward thirty to forty degrees, making the ideograph "eight," making the ideograph "human." Knees bent, I would swing into the slow, measured "square step," the powerful walk into battle. After five years my body became so strong that I could control even the dilations of the pupils inside my irises. I could copy owls and bats, the words for "bat" and "blessing" homonyms. After six years the deer let me run beside them. I could jump twenty feet into the air from a standstill, leaping like a monkey over the hut. Every creature has a hiding skill and a fighting skill a warrior can use. When birds alighted on my palm, I could yield my muscles under their feet and give them no base from which to fly away.

But I could not fly like the bird that led me here, except in large, free dreams.

During the seventh year (I would be fourteen), the two old people led me blindfolded to the mountains of the white tigers. They held me by either elbow and shouted into my ears, "Run. Run. Run." I ran and, not stepping off a cliff at the edge of my toes and not hitting my forehead against a wall, ran faster. A wind buoyed me up over the roots, the rocks, the little hills. We reached the tiger place in no time—a mountain peak three feet three from the sky. We had to bend over.

The old people waved once, slid down the mountain, and disappeared around a tree. The old woman, good with the bow and arrow, took them with her; the old man took the water gourd. I would have to survive bare-handed. Snow lay on the ground, and snow fell in loose gusts—another way the dragon breathes. I walked in the direction from which we had come, and when I reached the timberline, I collected wood broken from the cherry tree, the peony, and the walnut, which is the tree of life. Fire, the old people had taught me, is stored in trees that grow red flowers or red berries in the spring or whose leaves turn red in the fall. I took the wood from the protected spots beneath the trees and wrapped it in my scarf to keep dry. I dug where squirrels might have come, stealing one or two nuts at each place. These I also wrapped in my scarf. It is possible, the old people said, for a human being to live for fifty days on water. I would save the roots and nuts for hard climbs, the places where nothing grew, the emergency should I not find the hut. This time there would be no bird to follow.

The first night I burned half of the wood and slept curled against the mountain. I heard the white tigers prowling on the other side of the fire, but I could not distinguish them from the snow patches. The morning rose perfectly.

I hurried along, again collecting wood and edibles. I ate nothing and only drank the snow my fires made run.

The first two days were gifts, the fasting so easy to do, I so smug in my strength that on the third day, the hardest, I caught myself sitting on the ground, opening the scarf and staring at the nuts and dry roots. Instead of walking steadily on or even eating, I faded into dreams about the meat meals my mother used to cook, my monk's food forgotten. That night I burned up most of the wood I had collected, unable to sleep for facing my death—if not death here, then death someday. The moon animals that did not hibernate came out to hunt, but I had given up the habits of a carnivore since living with the old people. I would not trap the mice that danced so close or the owls that plunged just outside the fire.

On the fourth and fifth days, my eyesight sharp with hunger, I saw deer and used their trails when our ways coincided. Where the deer nibbled, I gathered the fungus, the fungus of immortality.

At noon on the tenth day I packed snow, white as rice, into the worn center of a rock pointed out to me by a finger of ice, and around the rock I built a fire. In the warming water I put roots, nuts, and the fungus of immortality. For variety I ate a quarter of the nuts and roots raw. Oh, green joyous rush inside my mouth, my head, my stomach, my toes, my soul—the best meal of my life.

One day I found that I was striding long distances without hindrance, my bundle light. Food had become so scarce that I was no longer stopping to collect it. I had walked into dead land. Here even the snow stopped. I did not go back to the richer areas, where I could not stay anyway, but, resolving to fast until I got halfway to the next woods, I started across the dry rocks. Heavily weighed down by the wood on my back, branches poking maddeningly, I had burned almost all of the fuel not to waste strength lugging it.

Somewhere in the dead land I lost count of the days. It

seemed as if I had been walking forever; life had never been different from this. An old man and an old woman were help I had only wished for. I was fourteen years old and lost from my village. I was walking in circles. Hadn't I been already found by the old people? Or was that yet to come? I wanted my mother and father. The old man and old woman were only a part of this lostness and this hunger.

One nightfall I ate the last of my food but had enough sticks for a good fire. I stared into the flames, which reminded me about helping my mother with the cooking and made me cry. It was very strange looking through water into fire and seeing my mother again. I nodded, orange and warm.

A white rabbit hopped beside me, and for a moment I thought it was a blob of snow that had fallen out of the sky. The rabbit and I studied each other. Rabbits taste like chickens. My mother and father had taught me how to hit rabbits over the head with wine jugs, then skin them cleanly for fur vests. "It's a cold night to be an animal," I said. "So you want some fire too, do you? Let me put on another branch, then." I would not hit it with the branch. I had learned from rabbits to kick backward. Perhaps this one was sick because normally the animals did not like fire. The rabbit seemed alert enough, however, looking at me so acutely, bounding up to the fire. But it did not stop when it got to the edge. It turned its face once toward me, then jumped into the fire. The fire went down for a moment, as if crouching in surprise, then the flames shot up taller than before. When the fire became calm again, I saw the rabbit had turned into meat, browned just right. I ate it, knowing the rabbit had sacrificed itself for me. It had made me a gift of meat.

When you have been walking through trees hour after hour—and I finally reached trees after the dead land—branches cross out everything, no relief whichever way your head turns until your eyes start to invent new sights. Hunger also changes the world—when eating can't be a habit, then neither can seeing. I saw two people made of gold dancing the earth's dances. They turned so perfectly that together they were the axis of the earth's turning. They were light; they were molten, changing gold—Chinese lion dancers, African lion dancers in midstep. I heard high Javanese bells deepen in midring to Indian bells, Hindu Indian, American Indian. Before my eyes, gold bells shredded into gold tassels that fanned into two royal capes that softened into lions' fur. Manes grew tall into feathers that shone—became light rays. Then the dancers danced the future—a machine-future—in clothes I had never seen before. I am watching the centuries pass in moments because suddenly I understand time, which is spinning and fixed like the North Star. And I understand how working and hoeing are dancing; how peasant clothes are golden, as king's clothes are golden; how one of the dancers is always a man and the other a woman.

The man and the woman grow bigger and bigger, so bright. All light. They are tall angels in two rows. They have high white wings on their backs. Perhaps there are infinite angels; perhaps I see two angels in their consecutive moments. I cannot bear their brightness and cover my eyes, which hurt from opening so wide without a blink. When I put my hands down to look again, I recognize the old brown man and the old gray woman walking toward me out of the pine forest.

It would seem that this small crack in the mystery was opened, not so much by the old people's magic, as by hunger. Afterward, whenever I did not eat for long, as during famine or battle, I could stare at ordinary people and see their light and gold. I could see their dance. When I get hungry enough, then killing and falling are dancing too.

The old people fed me hot vegetable soup. Then they asked me to talk-story about what happened in the mountains of the white tigers. I told them that the white tigers had stalked me through the snow but that I had fought them off with burning branches, and my great-grandparents had come to lead me safely through the forests. I had met a rabbit who taught me about self-immolation and how to speed up transmigration: one does not have to become worms first but can change directly into a human being— as in our own humaneness we had just changed bowls of vegetable soup into people too. That made them laugh. "You tell good stories," they said. "Now go to sleep, and tomorrow we will begin your dragon lessons."

"One more thing," I wanted to say. "I saw you and how old you really are." But I was already asleep; it came out only a murmur. I would want to tell them about that last moment of my journey; but it was only one moment out of the weeks that I had been gone, and its telling would keep till morning. Besides, the two people must already know. In the next years, when I suddenly came upon them or when I caught them out of the corners of my eyes, he appeared as a handsome young man, tall with long black hair, and she, as a beautiful young woman who ran bare-legged through the trees. In the spring she dressed like a bride; she wore juniper leaves in her hair and a black embroidered jacket. I learned to shoot accurately because my teachers held the targets. Often when sighting along an arrow, there to the side I would glimpse the young man or young woman, but when I looked directly, he or she would be old again. By this time I had guessed from their manner that the old woman was to the old man a sister or a friend rather than a wife.

After I returned from my survival test, the two old people trained me in dragon ways, which took another eight years. Copying the tigers, their stalking kill and their anger, had been a wild, bloodthirsty joy. Tigers are easy to find, but I needed adult wisdom to know dragons. "You have to infer the whole dragon from the parts you can see and touch," the old people would say. Unlike tigers, dragons are so immense, I would never see one in its entirety. But I could explore the mountains, which are the top of its head. "These mountains are also *like* the tops of *other* dragons' heads," the old people would tell me. When climbing the slopes, I could understand that I was a bug riding on a dragon's forehead as it roams through space, its speed so different from my speed that I feel the dragon solid and immobile. In quarries I could see its strata, the dragon's veins and muscles; the minerals, its teeth and bones. I could touch the stones the old woman wore—its bone marrow. I had worked the soil, which is its flesh, and harvested the plants and climbed the trees, which are its hairs. I could listen to its voice in the thunder and feel its breathing in the winds, see its breathing in the clouds. Its tongue is the lightning. And the red that the lightning gives to the world is strong and lucky—in blood, poppies, roses, rubies, the red feathers of birds, the red carp, the cherry tree, the peony, the line alongside the turtle's eyes and the mallard's. In the spring when the dragon awakes, I watched its turnings in the rivers.

The closest I came to seeing a dragon whole was when the old people cut away a small strip of bark on a pine that was over three thousand years old. The resin underneath flows in the swirling shapes of dragons. "If you should decide during your old age that you would like to live another five hundred years, come here and drink ten pounds of this sap," they told me. "But don't do it now. You're too young to decide to live forever." The old people sent me out into thunderstorms to pick the red-cloud herb, which grows only then, a product of dragon's fire and dragon's rain. I brought the leaves to the old man and old woman, and they ate them for immortality.

I learned to make my mind large, as the universe is large, so that there is room for paradoxes. Pearls are bone marrow; pearls come from oysters. The dragon lives in the sky, ocean, marshes, and mountains; and the mountains are also its cranium. Its voice thunders and jingles like copper pans. It breathes fire and water; and sometimes the dragon is one, sometimes many.

I worked every day. When it rained, I exercised in the downpour, grateful not to be pulling sweet potatoes. I moved like the trees in the wind. I was grateful not to be squishing in chicken mud, which I did not have nightmares about so frequently now.

On New Year's mornings, the old man let me look in his water gourd to see my family. They were eating the biggest meal of the year, and I missed them very much. I had felt loved, love pouring from their fingers when the adults tucked red money in our pockets. My two old people did not give me money, but, each year for fifteen years, a bead. After I unwrapped the red paper and rolled the bead about between thumb and fingers, they took it back for safekeeping. We ate monk's food as usual.

By looking into the water gourd I was able to follow the men I would have to execute. Not knowing that I watched, fat men ate meat; fat men drank wine made from the rice; fat men sat on naked little girls. I watched powerful men count their money, and starving men count theirs. When bandits brought their share of raids home, I waited until they took off their masks so I would know the villagers who stole from their neighbors. I studied the generals' faces, their rank-stalks quivering at the backs of their heads. I learned rebels' faces, too, their foreheads tied with wild oaths.

The old man pointed out strengths and weaknesses whenever heroes met in classical battles, but warfare makes a scramble of the beautiful, slow old fights. I saw one young fighter salute his opponent—and five peasants hit him from behind with scythes and hammers. His opponent did not warn him.

"Cheaters!" I yelled. "How am I going to win against cheaters?"

"Don't worry," the old man said. "You'll never be trapped like that poor amateur. You can see behind you like a bat. Hold the peasants back with one hand and kill the warrior with the other."

Menstrual days did not interrupt my training; I was as strong as on any other day. "You're now an adult," explained the old woman on the first one, which happened halfway through my stay on the mountain. "You can have children." I had thought I had cut myself when jumping over my swords, one made of steel and the other carved out of a single block of jade. "However," she added, "we are asking you to put off children for a few more years."

"Then can I use the control you taught me and stop this bleeding?"

"No. You don't stop shitting and pissing," she said. "It's the same with the blood. Let it run." ("Let it walk" in Chinese.)

To console me for being without family on this day, they let me look inside the gourd. My whole family was visiting friends on the other side of the river. Everybody had on good clothes and was exchanging cakes. It was a wedding. My mother was talking to the hosts: "Thank you for taking our daughter. Wherever she is, she must be happy now. She will certainly come back if she is alive, and if she is a spirit, you have given her a descent line. We are so grateful."

Yes, I would be happy. How full I would be with all their love for me. I would have for a new husband my own playmate, dear since childhood, who loved me so much he was to become a spirit bridegroom for my sake. We will be so happy when I come back to the valley, healthy and strong and not a ghost.

The water gave me a close-up of my husband's wonderful face—and I was watching when it went white at the sudden approach of armored men on horseback, thudding and jangling. My people grabbed iron skillets, boiling soup, knives, hammers, scissors, whatever weapons came to hand, but my father said, "There are too many of them," and they put down the weapons and waited quietly at the door, open as if for guests. An army of horsemen stopped at our house; the foot soldiers in the distance were coming closer. A horseman with silver scales afire in the sun shouted from the scroll in his hands, his words opening a red gap in his black beard. "Your baron has pledged fifty men from this district, one from each family," he said, and then named the family names.

"No!" I screamed into the gourd.

"I'll go," my new husband and my youngest brother said to their fathers.

"No," my father said, "I myself will go," but the women held him back until the foot soldiers passed by, my husband and my brother leaving with them.

As if disturbed by the marching feet, the water churned; and when it stilled again ("Wait!" I yelled. "Wait!"), there were strangers. The baron and his family —all of his family—were knocking their heads on the floor in front of their ancestors and thanking the gods out loud for protecting them from conscription. I watched the baron's piggish face chew open-mouthed on the sacrificial pig. I plunged my hand into the gourd, making a grab for his thick throat, and he broke into pieces, splashing water all over my face and clothes. I turned the gourd upside-down to empty it, but no little people came tumbling out.

"Why can't I go down there now and help them?" I cried. "I'll run away with the two boys and we'll hide in the caves."

"No," the old man said. "You're not ready. You're only fourteen years old. You'd get hurt for nothing."

"Wait until you are twenty-two," the old woman said. "You'll be big then and more skillful. No army will be able to stop you from doing whatever you want. If you go now, you will be killed, and you'll have wasted seven and a half years of our time. You will deprive your people of a champion."

"I'm good enough now to save the boys."

"We didn't work this hard to save just two boys, but whole families."

Of course.

"Do you really think I'll be able to do that—defeat an army?"

"Even when you fight against soldiers trained as you are, most of them will be men, heavy footed and rough. You will have the advantage. Don't be impatient."

"From time to time you may use the water gourd to watch your husband and your brother," the old man said.

But I had ended the panic about them already. I could feel a wooden door inside of me close. I had learned on the farm that I could stop loving animals raised for slaughter. And I could start loving them immediately when someone said, "This one is a pet," freeing me and opening the door. We had lost males before, cousins and uncles who were conscripted into armies or bonded as apprentices, who are almost as lowly as slave girls.

I bled and thought about the people to be killed; I bled and thought about the people to be born.

During all my years on the mountain, I talked to no one except the two old people, but they seemed to be many people. The whole world lived inside the gourd, the earth a green and blue pearl like the one the dragon plays with.

When I could point at the sky and make a sword appear, a silver bolt in the sunlight, and control its slashing with my mind, the old people said I was ready to leave. The old man opened the gourd for the last time. I saw the baron's messenger leave our house, and my father was saying, "This time I must go and fight." I would hurry down the mountain and take his place. The old people gave me the fifteen beads, which I was to use if I got into terrible danger. They gave me men's clothes and armor. We bowed to one another. The bird flew above me down the mountain, and for some miles, whenever I turned to look for them, there would be the two old people waving. I saw them through the mist; I saw them on the clouds; I saw them big on the mountaintop when distance had shrunk the pines. They had probably left images of themselves for me to wave at and gone about their other business.

When I reached my village, my father and mother had grown as old as the two whose shapes I could at last no longer see. I helped my parents carry their tools, and they walked ahead so straight, each carrying a basket or a hoe not to overburden me, their tears falling privately. My family surrounded me with so much love that I almost forgot the ones not there. I praised the new infants.

"Some of the people are saying the Eight Sages took

you away to teach you magic," said a little girl cousin. "They say they changed you into a bird, and you flew to them."

"Some say you went to the city and became a prostitute," another cousin giggled.

"You might tell them that I met some teachers who were willing to teach me science," I said.

"I have been drafted," my father said.

"No, Father," I said. "I will take your place."

My parents killed a chicken and steamed it whole, as if they were welcoming home a son, but I had gotten out of the habit of meat. After eating rice and vegetables, I slept for a long time, preparation for the work ahead.

In the morning my parents woke me and asked that I come with them to the family hall. "Stay in your nightclothes," my mother said. "Don't change yet." She was holding a basin, a towel, and a kettle of hot water. My father had a bottle of wine, an ink block and pens, and knives of various sizes. "Come with us," he said. They had stopped the tears with which they had greeted me. Forebodingly I caught a smell—metallic, the iron smell of blood, as when a woman gives birth, as at the sacrifice of a large animal, as when I menstruated and dreamed red dreams.

My mother put a pillow on the floor before the ancestors. "Kneel here," she said. "Now take off your shirt." I kneeled with my back to my parents so none of us felt embarrassed. My mother washed my back as if I had left for only a day and were her baby yet. "We are going to carve revenge on your back," my father said. "We'll write out oaths and names."

"Wherever you go, whatever happens to you, people will know our sacrifice," my mother said. "And you'll never forget either." She meant that even if I got killed, the people could use my dead body for a weapon, but we do not like to talk out loud about dying.

My father first brushed the words in ink, and they fluttered down my back row after row. Then he began cutting; to make fine lines and points he used thin blades, for the stems, large blades.

My mother caught the blood and wiped the cuts with a cold towel soaked in wine. It hurt terribly—the cuts sharp; the air burning; the alcohol cold, then hot—pain so various. I gripped my knees. I released them. Neither tension nor relaxation helped. I wanted to cry. If not for the fifteen years of training, I would have writhed on the floor; I would have had to be held down. The list of grievances went on and on. If an enemy should flay me, the light would shine through my skin like lace.

At the end of the last word, I fell forward. Together my parents sang what they had written, then let me rest. My mother fanned my back. "We'll have you with us until your back heals," she said.

When I could sit up again, my mother brought two mirrors, and I saw my back covered entirely with words in red and black files, like an army, like my army. My parents nursed me just as if I had fallen in battle after many victories. Soon I was strong again.

A white horse stepped into the courtyard where I was polishing my armor. Though the gates were locked tight, through the moon door it came—a kingly white horse. It wore a saddle and bridle with red, gold, and black tassles dancing. The saddle was just my size with tigers and dragons tooled in swirls. The white horse pawed the ground for me to go. On the hooves of its near forefoot and hindfoot was the ideograph "to fly."

My parents and I had waited for such a sign. We took the fine saddlebags off the horse and filled them with salves and herbs, blue grass for washing my hair, extra sweaters, dried peaches. They gave me a choice of ivory or silver chopsticks. I took the silver ones because they were lighter. It was like getting wedding presents. The cousins and the villagers came bearing bright orange jams, silk dresses, silver embroidery scissors. They brought blue and white porcelain bowls filled with water and carp—the bowls painted with carp, fins like orange fire. I accepted all the gifts—the tables, the earthenware jugs—though I could not possibly carry them with me, and culled for travel only a small copper cooking bowl. I could cook in it and eat out of it and would not have to search for bowl-shaped rocks or tortoiseshells.

I put on my men's clothes and armor and tied my hair in a man's fashion. "How beautiful you look," the people said. "How beautiful she looks."

A young man stepped out of the crowd. He looked familiar to me, as if he were the old man's son, or the old man himself when you looked at him from the corners of your eyes.

"I want to go with you," he said.

"You will be the first soldier in my army," I told him.

I leapt onto my horse's back and marveled at the power and height it gave to me. Just then, galloping out of nowhere straight at me came a rider on a black horse. The villagers scattered except for my one soldier, who stood calmly in the road. I drew my sword. "Wait!" shouted the rider, raising weaponless hands. "Wait. I have travelled here to join you."

Then the villagers relinquished their real gifts to me—their sons. Families who had hidden their boys during the last conscription volunteered them now. I took the ones their families could spare and the ones with hero-fire in their eyes, not the young fathers and not those who would break hearts with their leaving.

We were better equipped than many founders of dynasties had been when they walked north to dethrone an emperor; they had been peasants like us. Millions of us had laid our hoes down on the dry ground and faced north. We sat in the fields, from which the dragon had withdrawn its moisture, and sharpened those hoes. Then, though it be ten thousand miles away, we walked to the palace. We would report to the emperor. The emperor, who sat facing south, must have been very frightened—peasants everywhere walking day and night toward the capital, toward Peiping. But the last emperors of dynasties must not have been facing in the right direction, for they would have seen us and not let us get this hungry. We would not have had to shout our grievances. The peasants would crown as emperor a farmer who knew the earth or a beggar who understood hunger.

"Thank you, Mother. Thank you, Father," I said before leaving. They had carved their names and address on me, and I would come back.

Often I walked beside my horse to travel abreast of my army. When we had to impress other armies—marauders, columns of refugees filing past one another, boy gangs following their martial arts teachers—I mounted and rode in front. The soldiers who owned horses and weapons would pose fiercely on my left and right. The small bands joined us, but sometimes armies of equal or larger strength would fight us. Then screaming a mighty scream and swinging two swords over my head, I charged the leaders; I released my bloodthirsty army and my straining war-horse. I guided the horse with my knees, freeing both hands for sword-work, spinning green and silver circles all around me.

I inspired my army, and I fed them. At night I sang to them glorious songs that came out of the sky and into my head. When I opened my mouth, the songs poured out and were loud enough for the whole encampment to hear; my army stretched out for a mile. We sewed red flags and tied the red scraps around arms, legs, horses' tails. We wore our red clothes so that when we visited a village, we would look as happy as for New Year's Day. Then people would want to join the ranks. My army did not rape, only taking food where there was an abundance. We brought order wherever we went.

When I won over a goodly number of fighters, I built up my army enough to attack fiefdoms and to pursue the enemies I had seen in the water gourd.

My first opponent turned out to be a giant, so much

bigger than the toy general I used to peep at. During the charge, I singled out the leader, who grew as he ran toward me. Our eyes locked until his height made me strain my neck looking up, my throat so vulnerable to the stroke of a knife that my eyes dropped to the secret death points on the huge body. First I cut off his leg with one sword swipe, as Chen Luan-feng had chopped the leg off the thunder god. When the giant stumped toward me, I cut off his head. Instantly he reverted to his true self, a snake, and slithered away hissing. The fighting around me stopped as the combatants' eyes and mouths opened wide in amazement. The giant's spells now broken, his soldiers, seeing that they had been led by a snake, pledged their loyalty to me.

In the stillness after battle I looked up at the mountaintops; perhaps the old man and woman were watching me and would enjoy my knowing it. They'd laugh to see a creature winking at them from the bottom of the water gourd. But on a green ledge above the battlefield I saw the giant's wives crying. They had climbed out of their palanquins to watch their husband fight me, and now they were holding each other weeping. They were two sisters, two tiny fairies against the sky, widows from now on. Their long undersleeves, which they had pulled out to wipe their tears, flew white mourning in the mountain wind. After a time, they got back into their sedan chairs, and their servants carried them away.

I led my army northward, rarely having to sidetrack; the emperor himself sent the enemies I was hunting chasing after me. Sometimes they attacked us on two or three sides; sometimes they ambushed me when I rode ahead. We would always win, Kuan Kung, the god of war and literature riding before me. I would be told of in fairy tales myself. I overheard some soldiers—and now there were many who had not met me—say that whenever we had been in danger of losing, I made a throwing gesture and the opposing army would fall, hurled across the battlefield. Hailstones as big as heads would shoot out of the sky and the lightning would stab like swords, but never at those on my side. "On *his* side," they said. I never told them the truth. Chinese executed women who disguised themselves as soldiers or students, no matter how bravely they fought or how high they scored on the examinations.

One spring morning I was at work in my tent repairing equipment, patching my clothes, and studying maps when a voice said, "General, may I visit you in your tent, please?" As if it were my own home, I did not allow strangers in my tent. And since I had no family with me, no one ever visited inside. Riverbanks, hillsides, the cool sloped rooms under the pine trees—China provides her soldiers with meeting places enough. I opened the tent flap. And there in the sunlight stood my own husband with arms full of wildflowers for me. "You are beautiful," he said, and meant it truly. "I have looked for you everywhere. I've been looking for you since the day that bird flew away with you." We were so pleased with each other, the childhood friend found at last, the childhood friend mysteriously grown up. "I followed you, but you skimmed over the rocks until I lost you."

"I've looked for you too," I said, the tent now snug around us like a secret house when we were kids. "Whenever I heard about a good fighter, I went to see if it were you," I said. "I saw you marry me. I'm so glad you married me."

He wept when he took off my shirt and saw the scar-words on my back. He loosened my hair and covered the words with it. I turned around and touched his face, loving the familiar first.

So for a time I had a partner—my husband and I, soldiers together just as when we were little soldiers playing in the village. We rode side by side into battle. When I became pregnant, during the last four months, I wore my armor altered so that I looked like a powerful, big man. As a fat man, I walked with the foot soldiers so as not to jounce the gestation. Now when I was naked, I was a strange human being indeed—words carved on my back and the baby large in front.

I hid from battle only once, when I gave birth to our baby. In dark and silver dreams I had seen him falling from the sky, each night closer to the earth, his soul a star. Just before labor began, the last star rays sank into my belly. My husband would talk to me and not go, though I said for him to return to the battlefield. He caught the baby, a boy, and put it on my breast. "What are we going to do with this?" he asked, holding up the piece of umbilical cord that had been closest to the baby.

"Let's tie it to a flagpole until it dries," I said. We had both seen the boxes in which our parents kept the dried cords of all their children. "This one was yours, and this yours," my mother would say to us brothers and sisters, and fill us with awe that she could remember.

We made a sling for the baby inside my big armor, and rode back into the thickest part of the fighting. The umbilical cord flew with the red flag and made us laugh. At night inside our own tent, I let the baby ride on my back. The sling was made of red satin and purple silk; the four paisley straps that tied across my breasts and around my waist ended in housewife's pockets lined with a coin, a seed, a nut, and a juniper leaf. At the back of the sling I had sewn a tiny quilted triangle, red at its center against two shades of green; it marked the baby's nape for luck. I walked bowed, and the baby warmed himself against me, his breathing in rhythm with mine, his heart beating like my heart.

When the baby was a month old, we gave him a name and shaved his head. For the full-month ceremony my husband had found two eggs, which we dyed red by boiling them with a flag. I peeled one and rolled it all over the baby's head, his eyes, his lips, off his bump of a nose, his cheeks, his dear bald head and fontanel. I had brought dried grapefruit peel in my saddlebag, and we also boiled that. We washed our heads and hands in the grapefruit water, dabbing it on the baby's forehead and hands. Then I gave my husband the baby and told him to take it to his family, and I gave him all the money we had taken on raids to take to my family. "Go now," I said, "before he is old enough to recognize me." While the blur is still in his eyes and the little fists shut tight like buds, I'll send my baby away from me. I altered my clothes and became again the slim young man. Only now I would get so lonely with the tent so empty that I slept outside.

My white horse overturned buckets and danced on them; it lifted full wine cups with its teeth. The strong soldiers lifted the horse in a wooden tub, while it danced to the stone drums and flute music. I played with the soldiers, throwing arrows into a bronze jar. But I found none of these antics as amusing as when I first set out on the road.

It was during this lonely time, when any high cry made the milk spill from my breasts, that I got careless. Wildflowers distracted me so that I followed them, picking one, then another, until I was alone in the woods. Out from behind trees, springing off branches came the enemy, their leader looming like a genie out of the water gourd. I threw fists and feet at them, but they were so many, they pinned me to the earth while their leader drew his sword. My fear shot forth—a quick, jabbing sword that slashed fiercely, silver flashes, quick cuts wherever my attention drove it. The leader stared at the palpable sword swishing unclutched at his men, then laughed aloud. As if signaled by his laughter, two more swords appeared in midair. They clanged against mine, and I felt metal vibrate inside my brain. I willed my sword to hit back and to go after the head that controlled the other swords. But the man fought well, hurting my brain. The swords opened and closed, scissoring madly, metal zinging along metal. Unable to leave my sky-sword to work itself, I would be watching the swords move like puppets when the genie yanked my hair back and held a dagger against my throat. "Aha!" he said. "What have we here?" He lifted the bead pouch out of my shirt and cut the string. I grabbed his arm, but one of his swords dived toward me, and I rolled out of the way. A horse galloped up, and he leapt on it, escaping into the forest, the beads in his fist. His swords fought behind him until I heard him shout, "I am here!" and they flew to his side. So I had done battle with the prince who had mixed the blood of his two sons with the metal he had used for casting his swords.

I ran back to my soldiers and gathered the fastest horsemen for pursuit. Our horses ran like the little white water horses in the surf. Across a plain we could see the enemy, a dustdevil rushing toward the horizon. Wanting to see, I focused my eyes as the eagles had taught me, and there the genie would be—shaking one bead out of the pouch and casting it at us. Nothing happened. No thunder, no earthquake that split open the ground, no hailstones big as heads.

"Stop!" I ordered my riders. "Our horses are exhausted, and I don't want to chase any farther south." The rest of the victories would be won on my own, slow and without shortcuts.

I stood on top of the last hill before Peiping and saw the roads below me flow like living rivers. Between roads the woods and plains moved too; the land was peopled—the Han people, the People of One Hundred Surnames, marching with one heart, our tatters flying. The depth and width of Joy were exactly known to me: the Chinese population. After much hardship a few of our millions had arrived together at the capital. We faced our emperor personally. We beheaded him, cleaned out the palace, and inaugurated the peasant who would begin the new order. In his rags he sat on the throne facing south, and we, a great red crowd, bowed to him three times. He commended some of us who were his first generals.

I told the people who had come with me that they were free to go home now, but since the Long Wall was so close, I would go see it. They could come along if they liked. So, loath to disband after such high adventures, we reached the northern boundary of the world, chasing Mongols en route.

I touched the Long Wall with my own fingers, running the edge of my hand between the stones, tracing the grooves the builders' hands had made. We lay our foreheads and our cheeks against the Long Wall and cried like the women who had come here looking for their men so long building the wall. In my travels north, I had not found my brother.

Carrying the news about the new emperor, I went home, where one more battle awaited me. The baron who had drafted my brother would still be bearing sway over our village. Having dropped my soldiers off at crossroads and bridges, I attacked the baron's stronghold alone. I jumped over the double walls and landed with swords drawn and knees bent, ready to spring. When no one accosted me, I sheathed the swords and walked about like a guest until I found the baron. He was counting his money, his fat ringed fingers playing over the abacus.

"Who are you? What do you want?" he said, encircling his profits with his arms. He sat square and fat like a god.

"I want your life in payment for your crimes against the villagers."

"I haven't done anything to you. All this is mine. I earned it. I didn't steal it from you. I've never seen you before in my life. Who are you?"

"I am a female avenger."

Then—heaven help him—he tried to be charming, to appeal to me man to man. "Oh, come now. Everyone takes the girls when he can. The families are glad to be rid of them. 'Girls are maggots in the rice.' 'It is more profitable to raise geese than daughters.' " He quoted to me the sayings I hated.

"Regret what you've done before I kill you," I said.

"I haven't done anything other men—even you— wouldn't have done in my place."

"You took away my brother."

"I free my apprentices."

"He was not an apprentice."

"China needs soldiers in wartime."

"You took away my childhood."

"I don't know what you're talking about. We've never met before. I've done nothing to you."

"You've done this," I said, and ripped off my shirt to show him my back. "You are responsible for this." When I saw his startled eyes at my breasts, I slashed him across the face and on the second stroke cut off his head.

I pulled my shirt back on and opened the house to the villagers. The baron's family and servants hid in closets and under beds. The villagers dragged them out into the courtyard, where they tried them next to the beheading machine. "Did you take my harvest so that my children had to eat grass?" a weeping farmer asked.

"I saw him steal seed grain," another testified.

"My family was hiding under the thatch on the roof when the bandits robbed our house, and we saw this one take off his mask." They spared those who proved they could be reformed. They beheaded the others. Their necks were collared in the beheading machine, which slowly clamped shut. There was one last-minute reprieve of a bodyguard when a witness shouted testimony just as the vise was pinching blood. The guard had but recently joined the household in exchange for a child hostage. A slow killing gives a criminal time to regret his crimes and think of the right words to prove he can change.

I searched the house, hunting out people for trial. I came upon a locked room. When I broke down the door, I found women, cowering, whimpering women. I heard shrill insect noises and scurrying. They blinked weakly at me like pheasants that have been raised in the dark for soft meat. The servants who walked the ladies had abandoned them, and they could not escape on their little bound feet. Some crawled away from me, using their elbows to pull themselves along. These women would not be good for anything. I called the villagers to come identify any daughters they wanted to take home, but no one claimed any. I gave each woman a bagful of rice, which they sat on. They rolled the bags to the road. They wandered away like ghosts. Later, it would be said, they turned into the band of swords-women who were a mercenary army. They did not wear men's clothes like me, but rode as women in black and red dresses. They bought up girl babies so that many poor families welcomed their visitations. When slave girls and daughters-in-law ran away, people would say they joined these witch amazons. They killed men and boys. I myself never encountered such women and could not vouch for their reality.

After the trials we tore down the ancestral tablets. "We'll use this great hall for village meetings," I announced. "Here we'll put on operas; we'll sing together and talk-story." We washed the courtyard; we exorcised the house with smoke and red paper. "This is a new year," I told the people, "the year one."

I went home to my parents-in-law and husband and son. My son stared, very impressed by the general he had seen in the parade, but his father said, "It's your mother. Go to your mother." My son was delighted that the shiny general was his mother too. She gave him her helmet to wear and her swords to hold.

Wearing my black embroidered wedding coat, I knelt at my parents-in-law's feet, as I would have done as a bride. "Now my public duties are finished," I said. "I will stay with you, doing farmwork and housework, and giving you more sons."

"Go visit your mother and father first," my mother-in-law said, a generous woman. "They want to welcome you."

My mother and father and the entire clan would be living happily on the money I had sent them. My parents had bought their coffins. They would sacrifice a pig to the gods that I had returned. From the words on my back, and how they were fulfilled, the villagers would make a legend about my perfect filiality.

My American life has been such a disappointment.

"I got straight A's, Mama."

"Let me tell you a true story about a girl who saved her village."

I could not figure out what was my village. And it was

important that I do something big and fine, or else my parents would sell me when we made our way back to China. In China there were solutions for what to do with little girls who ate up food and threw tantrums. You can't eat straight A's.

When one of my parents or the emigrant villagers said, "'Feeding girls is feeding cowbirds,'" I would thrash on the floor and scream so hard I couldn't talk. I couldn't stop.

"What's the matter with her?"

"I don't know. Bad, I guess. You know how girls are. 'There's no profit in raising girls. Better to raise geese than girls.'"

"I would hit her if she were mine. But then there's no use wasting all that discipline on a girl. 'When you raise girls, you're raising children for strangers.'"

"Stop that crying!" my mother would yell. "I'm going to hit you if you don't stop. Bad girl! Stop!" I'm going to remember never to hit or to scold my children for crying, I thought, because then they will only cry more.

"I'm not a bad girl," I would scream. "I'm not a bad girl. I'm not a bad girl." I might as well have said, "I'm not a girl."

"When you were little, all you had to say was 'I'm not a bad girl,' and you could make yourself cry," my mother says, talking-story about my childhood.

I minded that the emigrant villagers shook their heads at my sister and me. "One girl—and another girl," they said, and made our parents ashamed to take us out together. The good part about my brothers being born was that people stopped saying, "All girls," but I learned new grievances. "Did you roll an egg on *my* face like that when *I* was born?" "Did you have a full-month party for *me*?" "Did you turn on all the lights?" "Did you send *my* picture to Grandmother?" "Why not? Because I'm a girl? Is that why not?" "Why didn't you teach me English?" "You like having me beaten up at school, don't you?"

"She is very mean, isn't she?" the emigrant villagers would say.

"Come, children. Hurry. Hurry. Who wants to go out with Great-Uncle?" On Saturday mornings my great-uncle, the ex-river pirate, did the shopping. "Get your coats, whoever's coming."

"I'm coming. I'm coming. Wait for me."

When he heard girls' voices, he turned on us and roared, "No girls!" and left my sisters and me hanging our coats back up, not looking at one another. The boys came back with candy and new toys. When they walked through Chinatown, the people must have said, "A boy—and another boy— and another boy!" At my great-uncle's funeral I secretly tested out feeling glad that he was dead—the six-foot bearish masculinity of him.

I went away to college—Berkeley in the sixties—and I studied, and I marched to change the world, but I did not turn into a boy. I would have liked to bring myself back as a boy for my parents to welcome with chickens and pigs. That was for my brother, who returned alive from Vietnam.

If I went to Vietnam, I would not come back; females desert families. It was said, "There is an outward tendency in females," which meant that I was getting straight A's for the good of my future husband's family, not my own. I did not plan ever to have a husband. I would show my mother and father and the nosey emigrant villagers that girls have no outward tendency. I stopped getting straight A's.

And all the time I was having to turn myself American-feminine, or no dates.

There is a Chinese word for the female *I*—which is "slave." Break the women with their own tongues!

I refused to cook. When I had to wash dishes, I would crack one or two. "Bad girl," my mother yelled, and sometimes that made me gloat rather than cry. Isn't a bad girl almost a boy?

"What do you want to be when you grow up, little girl?"

"A lumberjack in Oregon."

Even now, unless I'm happy, I burn the food when I cook. I do not feed people. I let the dirty dishes rot. I eat at other people's tables but won't invite them to mine, where the dishes are rotting.

If I could not-eat, perhaps I could make myself a warrior like the swordswoman who drives me. I will—I must—rise and plow the fields as soon as the baby comes out.

Once I get outside the house, what bird might call me; on what horse could I ride away? Marriage and childbirth strengthen the swordswoman, who is not a maid like Joan of Arc. Do the women's work; then do more work, which will become ours too. No husband of mine will say, "I could have been a drummer, but I had to think about the wife and kids. You know how it is." Nobody supports me at the expense of his own adventure. Then I get bitter: no one supports me; I am not loved enough to be supported. That I am not a burden has to compensate for the sad envy when I look at women loved enough to be supported. Even now China wraps double binds around my feet.

When urban renewal tore down my parents' laundry and paved over our slum for a parking lot, I only made up gun and knife fantasies and did nothing useful.

From the fairy tales, I've learned exactly who the enemy are. I easily recognize them—business-suited in their modern American executive guise, each boss two feet taller than I am and impossible to meet eye to eye.

I once worked at an art supply house that sold paints to artists. "Order more of that nigger yellow, willya?" the boss told me. "Bright, isn't it? Nigger yellow."

"I don't like that word," I had to say in my bad, small-person's voice that makes no impact. The boss never deigned to answer.

I also worked at a land developers' association. The building industry was planning a banquet for contractors, real estate dealers, and real estate editors. "Did you know the restaurant you chose for the banquet is being picketed by CORE and the NAACP?" I squeaked.

"Of course I know." The boss laughed. "That's why I chose it."

"I refuse to type these invitations," I whispered, voice unreliable.

He leaned back in his leather chair, his bossy stomach opulent. He picked up his calendar and slowly circled a date. "You will be paid up to here," he said. "We'll mail you the check."

If I took the sword, which my hate must surely have forged out of the air, and gutted him, I would put color and wrinkles into his shirt.

It's not just the stupid racists that I have to do something about, but the tyrants who for whatever reason can deny my family food and work. My job is my own only land.

To avenge my family, I'd have to storm across China to take back our farm from the Communists; I'd have to rage across the United States to take back the laundry in New York and the one in California. Nobody in history has conquered and united both North America and Asia. A descendant of eighty pole fighters, I ought to be able to set out confidently, march straight down our street, get going right now. There's work to do, ground to cover. Surely, the eighty pole fighters, though unseen, would follow me and lead me and protect me, as is the wont of ancestors.

Or it may well be that they're resting happily in China, their spirits dispersed among the real Chinese, and not nudging me at all with their poles. I mustn't feel bad that I haven't done as well as the swordswoman did; after all, no bird called me, no wise old people tutored me. I have no magic beads, no water gourd sight, no rabbit that will jump in the fire when I'm hungry. I dislike armies.

I've looked for the bird. I've seen clouds make pointed angel wings that stream past the sunset, but they shred into clouds. Once at a beach after a long hike I saw a seagull, tiny as an insect. But when I jumped up to tell what miracle I saw, before I could get the words out I understood that the bird was insect-size because it was far away. My brain had momentarily lost its depth perception. I was that eager to find an unusual bird.

The news from China has been confusing. It also had something to do with birds. I was nine years old when the letters made my parents, who are rocks, cry. My father screamed in his sleep. My mother wept and crumpled up the letters. She set fire to them page by page in the ashtray, but new letters came almost every day. The only letters they opened without fear were the ones with red borders, the holiday letters that mustn't carry bad news. The other letters said that my uncles were made to kneel on broken glass during their trials and had confessed to being land-owners. They were all executed, and the aunt whose thumbs were twisted off drowned herself. Other aunts, mothers-in-law, and cousins disappeared; some suddenly began writing to us again from communes or from Hong Kong. They kept asking for money. The ones in communes got four ounces of fat and one cup of oil a week, they said, and had to work from 4 A.M. to 9 P.M. They had to learn to do dances waving red kerchiefs; they had to sing nonsense syllables. The Communists gave axes to the old ladies and said, "Go and kill yourself. You're useless." If we overseas Chinese would just send money to the Communist bank, our relatives said, they might get a percentage of it for themselves. The aunts in Hong Kong said to send money quickly; their children were begging on the sidewalks, and mean people put dirt in their bowls.

When I dream that I am wire without flesh, there is a letter on blue airmail paper that floats above the night ocean between here and China. It must arrive safely or else my grandmother and I will lose each other.

My parents felt bad whether or not they sent money. Sometimes they got angry at their brothers and sisters for asking. And they would not simply ask but have to talk-story too. The revolutionaries had taken Fourth Aunt and Uncle's store, house, and lands. They attacked the house and killed the grandfather and oldest daughter. The grandmother escaped with the loose cash and did not return to help. Fourth Aunt picked up her sons, one under each arm, and hid in the pig house, where they slept that night in cotton clothes. The next day she found her husband, who had also miraculously escaped. The two of them collected twigs and yams to sell while their children begged. Each morning they tied the faggots on each other's back. Nobody bought from them. They ate the yams and some of the children's rice. Finally Fourth Aunt saw what was wrong. "We have to shout 'Fuel for sale' and 'Yams for sale,' " she said. "We can't just walk unobtrusively up and down the street." "You're right," said my uncle, but he was shy and walked in back of her. "Shout," my aunt ordered, but he could not. "They think we're carrying these sticks home for our own fire," she said. "Shout." They walked about miserably, silently, until sundown, neither of them able to advertise themselves. Fourth Aunt, an orphan since the age of ten, mean as my mother, threw her bundle down at his feet and scolded Fourth Uncle, "Starving to death, his wife and children starving to death, and he's too damned shy to raise his voice." She left him standing by himself and afraid to return empty-handed to her. He sat under a tree to think, when he spotted a pair of nesting doves. Dumping his bag of yams, he climbed up and caught the birds. That was where the Communists trapped him, in the tree. They criticized him for selfishly taking food for his own family and killed him, leaving his body in the tree as an example. They took the birds to a commune kitchen to be shared.

It is confusing that my family was not the poor to be championed. They were executed like the barons in the stories, when they were not barons. It is confusing that birds tricked us.

What fighting and killing I have seen have not been glorious but slum grubby. I fought the most during junior high school and always cried. Fights are confusing as to who has won. The corpses I've seen had been rolled and dumped, sad little dirty bodies covered with a police khaki blanket. My mother locked her children in the house so we couldn't look at dead slum people. But at news of a body,

I would find a way to get out; I had to learn about dying if I wanted to become a swordswoman. Once there was an Asian man stabbed next door, words on cloth pinned to his corpse. When the police came around asking questions, my father said, "No read Japanese. Japanese words. Me Chinese."

I've also looked for old people who could be my gurus. A medium with red hair told me that a girl who died in a far country follows me wherever I go. This spirit can help me if I acknowledge her, she said. Between the head line and heart line in my right palm, she said, I have the mystic cross. I could become a medium myself. I don't want to be a medium. I don't want to be a crank taking "offerings" in a wicker plate from the frightened audience, who, one after another, asked the spirits how to raise rent money, how to cure their coughs and skin diseases, how to find a job. And martial arts are for unsure little boys kicking away under fluorescent lights.

I live now where there are Chinese and Japanese, but no emigrants from my own village looking at me as if I had failed them. Living among one's own emigrant villagers can give a good Chinese far from China glory and a place. "That old busboy is really a swordsman," we whisper when he goes by, "He's a swordsman who's killed fifty. He has a tong ax in his closet." But I am useless, one more girl who couldn't be sold. When I visit the family now, I wrap my American successes around me like a private shawl; I *am* worthy of eating the food. From afar I can believe my family loves me fundamentally. They only say, "When fishing for treasures in the flood, be careful not to pull in girls," because that is what one says about daughters. But I watched such words come out of my own mother's and father's mouths; I looked at their ink drawing of poor people snagging their neighbors' flotage with long flood hooks and pushing the girl babies on down the river. And I had to get out of hating range. I read in an anthropology book that Chinese say, "Girls are necessary too"; I have never heard the Chinese I know make this concession. Perhaps it was a saying in another village. I refuse to shy my way anymore through our Chinatown, which tasks me with the old sayings and the stories.

The swordswoman and I are not so dissimilar. May my people understand the resemblance soon so that I can return to them. What we have in common are the words at our backs. The idioms for *revenge* are "report a crime" and "report to five families." The reporting is the vengeance—not the beheading, not the gutting, but the words. And I have so many words—"chink" words and "gook" words too—that they do not fit on my skin.

Shaman

Once in a long while, four times so far for me, my mother brings out the metal tube that holds her medical diploma. On the tube are gold circles crossed with seven red lines each—"joy" ideographs in abstract. There are also little flowers that look like gears for a gold machine. According to the scraps of labels with Chinese and American addresses, stamps, and postmarks, the family airmailed the can from Hong Kong in 1950. It got crushed in the middle, and whoever tried to peel the labels off stopped because the red and gold paint came off too, leaving silver scratches that rust. Somebody tried to pry the end off before discovering that the tube pulls apart. When I open it, the smell of China flies out, a thousand-year-old bat flying heavy-headed out of the Chinese caverns where bats are as white as dust, a smell that comes from long ago, far back in the brain. Crates from Canton, Hong Kong, Singapore, and Taiwan have that smell too, only stronger because they are more recently come from the Chinese.

Inside the can are three scrolls, one inside another. The largest says that in the twenty-third year of the National Republic, the To Keung School of Midwifery, where she has had two years of instruction and Hospital Practice, awards its Diploma to my mother, who has shown through oral and written examination her Proficiency in Midwifery, Pediatrics, Gynecology, "Medecine," "Surgary," Therapeutics, Ophthalmology, Bacteriology, Dermatology, Nursing, and Bandage. This document has eight stamps on it: one, the school's English and Chinese names embossed together in a circle; one, as the Chinese enumerate, a stork and a big baby in lavender ink; one, the school's Chinese seal; one, an orangish paper stamp pasted in the border design; one, the red seal of Dr. Wu Pak-liang, M.D., Lyon, Berlin, president and "Ex-assistant étranger à la clinique chirugicale et d'accouchement de l'université de Lyon"; one, the red seal of Dean Woo Yin-kam, M.D.; one, my mother's seal, her chop mark larger than the president's and the dean's; and one, the number 1279 on the back. Dean Woo's signature is followed by "(Hackett)." I read in a history book that Hackett Medical College for Women at Canton was founded in the nineteenth century by European women doctors.

The school seal has been pressed over a photograph of my mother at the age of thirty-seven. The diploma gives her age as twenty-seven. She looks younger than I do, her eyebrows are thicker, her lips fuller. Her naturally curly hair is parted on the left, one wavy wisp tendrilling off to the right. She wears a scholar's white gown, and she is not thinking about her appearance. She stares straight ahead as if she could see me and past me to her grandchildren and grandchildren's grandchildren. She has spacy eyes, as all people recently from Asia have. Her eyes do not focus on the camera. My mother is not smiling; Chinese do not smile for photographs. Their faces command relatives in foreign lands—"Send money"—and posterity forever—"Put food in front of this picture." My mother does not understand Chinese-American snapshots. "What are you laughing at?" she asks.

The second scroll is a long narrow photograph of the graduating class with the school officials seated in front. I picked out my mother immediately. Her face is exactly her own, though forty years younger. She is so familiar, I can only tell whether or not she is pretty or happy or smart by comparing her to the other women. For this formal group picture she straightened her hair with oil to make a chin-length bob like the others'. On the other women, strangers, I can recognize a curled lip, a sidelong glance, pinched shoulders. My mother is not soft; the girl with the small nose and dimpled underlip is soft. My mother is not humorous, not like the girl at the end who lifts her mocking chin to pose like Girl Graduate. My mother does not have smiling eyes; the old woman teacher (Dean Woo?) in front crinkles happily, and the one faculty member in the western suit smiles westernly. Most of the graduates are girls whose faces have not yet formed; my mother's face will not change anymore, except to age. She is intelligent, alert, pretty. I can't tell if she's happy.

The graduates seem to have been looking elsewhere when they pinned the rose, zinnia, or chrysanthemum on their precise black dresses. One thin girl wears hers in the middle of her chest. A few have a flower over a left or a right nipple. My mother put hers, a chrysanthemum, below her left breast. Chinese dresses at that time were dartless, cut as if women did not have breasts; these young doctors, unaccustomed to decorations, may have seen their chests as black expanses with no reference points for flowers. Perhaps they couldn't shorten that far gaze that lasts only a few years after a Chinese emigrates. In this picture too my mother's eyes are big with what they held—reaches of oceans beyond China, land beyond oceans. Most emigrants learn the barbarians' directness—how to gather themselves and stare rudely into talking faces as if trying to catch lies. In America my mother has eyes as strong as boulders, never once skittering off a face, but she has not learned to place decorations and phonograph needles, nor has she stopped seeing land on the other side of the oceans. Now her eyes include the relatives in China, as they once included my father smiling and smiling in his many western outfits, a different one for each photograph that he sent from America.

He and his friends took pictures of one another in bathing suits at Coney Island beach, the salt wind from the Atlantic blowing their hair. He's the one in the middle with his arms about the necks of his buddies. They pose in the cockpit of a biplane, on a motorcycle, and on a lawn beside the "Keep Off the Grass" sign. They are always laughing.

My father, white shirt sleeves rolled up, smiles in front of a wall of clean laundry. In the spring he wears a new straw hat, cocked at a Fred Astaire angle. He steps out, dancing down the stairs, one foot forward, one back, a hand in his pocket. He wrote to her about the American custom of stomping on straw hats come fall. "If you want to save your hat for next year," he said, "you have to put it away early, or else when you're riding the subway or walking along Fifth Avenue, any stranger can snatch it off your head and put his foot through it. That's the way they celebrate the change of seasons here." In the winter he wears a gray felt hat with his gray overcoat. He is sitting on a rock in Central Park. In one snapshot he is not smiling; someone took it when he was studying, blurred in the glare of the desk lamp.

There are no snapshots of my mother. In two small portraits, however, there is a black thumbprint on her forehead, as if someone had inked in bangs, as if someone had marked her.

"Mother, did bangs come into fashion after you had the picture taken?" One time she said yes. Another time when I asked, "Why do you have fingerprints on your forehead?" she said, "Your First Uncle did that." I disliked the unsureness in her voice.

The last scroll has columns of Chinese words. The only English is "Department of Health, Canton," imprinted on my mother's face, the same photograph as on the diploma. I keep looking to see whether she was afraid. Year after year my father did not come home or send for her. Their two children had been dead for ten years. If he did not return soon, there would be no more children. ("They were three and two years old, a boy and a girl. They could talk already.") My father did send money regularly, though, and she had nobody to spend it on but herself. She bought good clothes and shoes. Then she decided to use the money for becoming a doctor. She did not leave for Canton immediately after the children died. In China there was time to complete feelings. As my father had done, my mother left the village by ship. There was a sea bird painted on the ship to protect it against shipwreck and winds. She was in luck. The following ship was boarded by river pirates, who kidnapped every passenger, even old ladies. "Sixty dollars for an old lady" was what the bandits used to say. "I sailed alone," she says, "to the capital of the entire province." She took a brown leather suitcase and a seabag stuffed with two quilts.

At the dormitory the school official assigned her to a room with five other women, who were unpacking when she came in. They greeted her and she greeted them. But no one wanted to start friendships until the unpacking was done, each item placed precisely to section off the room. My mother spotted the name she had written on her application pinned to a headboard, and the annoyance she felt at not arriving early enough for first choice disappeared. The locks on her suitcase opened with two satisfying clicks; she enjoyed again how neatly her belongings fitted together, clean against the green lining. She refolded the clothes before putting them in the one drawer that was hers. Then she took out her pens and inkbox, an atlas of the world, a tea set and tea cannister, sewing box, her ruler with the real gold markings, writing paper, envelopes with the thick red stripe to signify no bad news, her bowl and silver chopsticks. These things she arranged one by one on her shelf. She spread the two quilts on top of the bed and put her slippers side by side underneath. She owned more—furniture, wedding jewelry, cloth, photographs—but she had left such troublesome valuables behind in the family's care. She never did get all of it back.

The women who had arrived early did not offer to help unpack, not wanting to interfere with the pleasure and the privacy of it. Not many women got to live out the daydream of women—to have a room, even a section of a room, that only gets messed up when she messes it up herself. The book would stay open at the very page she had pressed flat with her hand, and no one would complain about the field not being plowed or the leak in the roof. She would clean her own bowl and a small, limited area; she would have one drawer to sort, one bed to make.

To shut the door at the end of the workday, which does not spill over into evening. To throw away books after reading them so they don't have to be dusted. To go through boxes on New Year's Eve and throw out half of what is inside. Sometimes for extravagance to pick a bunch of flowers for the one table. Other women besides me must have this daydream about a carefree life. I've seen Communist pictures showing a contented woman sitting on her bunk sewing. Above her head is her one box on a shelf. The words stenciled on the box mean "Fragile," but literally say, "Use a little heart." The woman looks very pleased. The Revolution put an end to prostitution by giving women what they wanted: a job and a room of their own.

Free from families, my mother would live for two years without servitude. She would not have to run errands for my father's tyrant mother with the bound feet or thread needles for the old ladies, but neither would there be slaves and nieces to wait on her. Now she would get hot water only if she bribed the concierge. When I went away to school my mother said, "Give the concierge oranges."

Two of my mother's roommates, who had organized their corners to their satisfaction, made tea and set a small table with their leftover travel food. "Have you eaten, Lady Scholar?" they invited my mother. "Lady Scholar, come drink tea," they said to each of the others. "Bring your own cup." This largess moved my mother—tea, an act of humility. She brought out meats and figs she had preserved on the farm. Everyone complimented her on their tastiness. The women told which villages they came from and the names they would go by. My mother did not let it be known that she had already had two children and that some of these girls were young enough to be her daughters.

Then everyone went to the auditorium for two hours of speeches by the faculty. They told the students that they would begin with a text as old as the Han empire, when the prescription for immortality had not yet been lost. Chang

Chung-ching, father of medicine, had told how the two great winds, *yang* and *yin*, blew through the human body. The diligent students would do well to begin tonight memorizing his book on colds and fevers. After they had mastered the ancient cures that worked, they would be taught the most up-to-date western discoveries. By the time the students graduated—those of them who persevered—their range of knowledge would be wider than that of any other doctor in history. Women have now been practicing medicine for about fifty years, said one of the teachers, a woman, who complimented them for adding to their growing number and also for coming to a school that taught modern medicine. "You will bring science to the villages." At the end of the program, the faculty turned their backs to the students, and everyone bowed the three bows toward the picture of Doctor Sun Yat-sen, who was a western surgeon before he became a revolutionary. Then they went to the dining hall to eat. My mother began memorizing her books immediately after supper.

There were two places where a student could study: the dining hall with its tables cleared for work, everyone chanting during the common memorization sessions; or the table in her own room. Most students went to the dining hall for the company there. My mother usually stayed in her room or, when a roommate wanted the privacy of it also, went to a secret hiding place she had hunted out during the first week of school. Once in a while she dropped by the dining hall, chanted for a short while with the most advanced group, not missing a syllable, yawned early, and said good-night. She quickly built a reputation for being brilliant, a natural scholar who could glance at a book and know it.

"The other students fought over who could sit next to me at exams," says my mother. "One glimpse at my paper when they got stuck, and they could keep going."

"Did you ever try to stop them from copying your paper?"

"Of course not. They only needed to pick up a word or

two, and they could remember the rest. That's not copying. You get a lot more clues in actual diagnosis. Patients talk endlessly about their ailments. I'd feel their pulses knocking away under my very fingertips—so much clearer than the paperdolls in the textbooks. I'd chant the symptoms, and those few words would start a whole chapter of cures tumbling out. Most people don't have the kind of brains that can do that." She pointed at the photograph of the thirty-seven graduates. "One hundred and twelve students began the course at the same time I did."

She suspected she did not have the right kind of brains either, my father the one who can recite whole poems. To make up the lack, she did secret studying. She also gave herself twenty years' headstart over the young girls, although she admitted to only ten, which already forced her to push. Older people were expected to be smarter; they are closer to the gods. She did not want to overhear students or teachers say, "She must be exceedingly stupid, doing no better than anyone else when she is a generation older. She's so dumb, she has to study day and night."

"I studied far in advance," says my mother. "I studied when the breathing coming from the beds and coming through the wood walls was deep and even. The night before exams, when the other students stayed up, I went to bed early. They would say, 'Aren't you going to study?' and I'd say, 'No, I'm going to do some mending,' or, 'I want to write letters tonight.' I let them take turns sitting next to me at the tests." The sweat of hard work is not to be displayed. It is much more graceful to appear favored by the gods.

Maybe my mother's secret place was the room in the dormitory which was haunted. Even though they had to crowd the other rooms, none of the young women would sleep in it. Accustomed to nestling with a bedful of siblings and grannies, they fitted their privacy tighter rather than claim the haunted room as human territory. No one had lived in it for at least five years, not since a series of hauntings had made its inhabitants come down with ghost fear that shattered their brains for studying. The haunted ones would give high, startled cries, pointing at the air, which sure enough was becoming hazy. They would suddenly turn and go back the way they had come. When they rounded a corner, they flattened themselves fast against the building to catch what followed unawares moving steadily forward. One girl tore up the photographs she had taken of friends in that room. The stranger with arms hanging at its sides who stood beside the wall in the background of the photograph was a ghost. The girl would insist there had been nobody there when she took the picture. "That was a Photo Ghost," said my mother when the students talked-story. "She needn't have been afraid. Most ghosts are only nightmares. Somebody should have held her and wiggled her ears to wake her up."

My mother relished these scare orgies. She was good at naming—Wall Ghost, Frog Spirit (frogs are "heavenly chickens"), Eating Partner. She could find descriptions of phenomena in ancient writings—the Green Phoenix stories, "The Seven Strange Tales of the Golden Bottle," "What Confucius Did Not Talk About." She could validate ghost sightings.

"But ghosts can't be just nightmares," a storyteller protested. "They come right out into the room. Once our whole family saw wine cups spinning and incense sticks waving through the air. We got the magic monk to watch all night. He also saw the incense tips tracing orange figures in the dark—ideographs, he said. He followed the glow patterns with his inkbrush on red paper. And there it was, a message from our great-grandfather. We needed to put bigger helpings and a Ford in front of his plaque. And when we did, the haunting stopped immediately."

"I like to think the ancestors are busier than that," my mother said, "or more at rest. Yes, they're probably more at rest. Perhaps it was an animal spirit that was bothering your house, and your grandfather had something to do with chasing it off." After what she thought was a suitably tactful pause, she said, "How do we know that ghosts are the continuance of dead people? Couldn't ghosts be an entirely different species of creature? Perhaps human beings just die, and that's the end. I don't think I'd mind that too much. Which would you rather be? A ghost who is constantly wanting to be fed? Or nothing?"

If the other storytellers had been reassuring one another with science, then my mother would have flown stories as factual as bats into the listening night. A practical woman, she could not invent stories and told only true ones. But tonight the younger women were huddling together under the quilts, the ghost room with its door open steps away.

"Did you hear that?" someone would whisper. And sure enough, whenever their voices stilled simultaneously, a thump or a creak would unmistakably sound somewhere inside the building. The girls would jump closer together giggling.

"That was the wind," my mother would say. "That was somebody who fell asleep reading in bed; she dropped her book." She neither jumped nor giggled.

"If you're so sure," said an impertinent girl, perhaps the one with the disdainful chin, "why don't you go out there and take a look?"

"Of course," said my mother. "I was just thinking about doing that," and she took a lamp and left her friends, impressed, in a dimmer room. She advanced steadily, waking the angular shadows up and down the corridor. She walked to both ends of the hallway, then explored another wing for good measure. At the ghost room, door open like a mouth, she stopped and, stepping inside, swung light into its corners. She saw cloth bags in knobby mounds; they looked like gnomes but were not gnomes. Suitcases and boxes threw shadow stairs up the walls and across the floor. Nothing unusual loomed at her or scurried away. No temperature change, no smell.

She turned her back on the room and slowly walked through one more wing. She did not want to get back too soon. Her friends, although one owes nothing to friends, must be satisfied that she searched thoroughly. After a sufficiently brave time, she returned to the storytellers. "I saw nothing," she said. "There's nothing to be afraid of in the whole dormitory, including the ghost room. I checked there too. I went inside just now."

"The haunting begins at midnight," said the girl with the adamantine chin. "It's not quite eleven."

My mother may have been afraid, but she would be a dragoness ("my totem, your totem"). She could make herself not weak. During danger she fanned out her dragon claws and riffled her red sequin scales and unfolded her coiling green stripes. Danger was a good time for showing off. Like the dragons living in temple eaves, my mother looked down on plain people who were lonely and afraid.

"I'm so sleepy," my mother said. "I don't want to wait up until midnight. I'll go sleep in the ghost room. Then if anything happens, I won't miss it. I hope I'll be able to recognize the ghost when I see it. Sometimes ghosts put on such mundane disguises, they aren't particularly interesting."

"Aiaa. Aiaa," the storytellers exclaimed. My mother laughed with satisfaction at their cries.

"I'll call out if something bad happens to me," she said. "If you come running all together, you will probably be able to scare any ghost away."

Some of them promised to come; some offered their talismans—a branch from a peach tree, a Christian cross, a red paper with good words written on it. But my mother refused them all. "If I take charms, then the ghost will hide from me. I won't learn what kind of ghost it is, or whether or not a ghost lives in there at all. I'll only bring a knife to defend myself and a novel in case I get bored and can't sleep. You keep the charms; should I call for help, bring them with you." She went to her own room and got weapon and book, though not a novel but a textbook.

Two of her roommates walked her to the ghost room. "Aren't you afraid?" they asked.

"What is there to be afraid of?" she asked. "What could

a ghost do to me?" But my mother did pause at the door. "Listen," she said, "if I am very afraid when you find me, don't forget to tweak my ears. Call my name and tell me how to get home." She told them her personal name.

She walked directly to the back of the room, where the boxes formed a windowseat. She sat with the lamp beside her and stared at her yellow and black reflection in the night glass. "I am very pretty," she thought. She cupped her hands to the window to see out. A thin moon pricked through the clouds, and the long grass waved. "That is the same moon that they see in New Society Village," she thought, "the same stars." ("That is the same moon that they see in China, the same stars though shifted a little.")

When she set the lamp next to the bed, the room seemed darker, the uncurtained window letting in the bare night. She wrapped herself well in her quilt, which her mother had made before dying young. In the middle of one border my grandmother had sewn a tiny satin triangle, a red heart to protect my mother at the neck, as if she were her baby yet.

My mother read aloud; perhaps the others could hear how calmly. The ghost might hear her too; she did not know whether her voice would evoke it or disperse it. Soon the ideographs lifted their feet, stretched out their wings, and flew like blackbirds; the dots were their eyes. Her own eyes drooped. She closed her book and turned off the lamp.

A new darkness pulled away the room, inked out flesh and outlined bones. My mother was wide awake again. She became sharply herself—bone, wire, antenna—but she was not afraid. She had been pared down like this before, when she had travelled up the mountains into rare snow—alone in white not unlike being alone in black. She had also sailed a boat safely between land and land.

She did not know whether she had fallen asleep or not when she heard a rushing coming out from under the bed. Cringes of fear seized her soles as something alive, rumbling, climbed the foot of the bed. It rolled over her and landed bodily on her chest. There it sat. It breathed airlessly, pressing her, sapping her. "Oh, no. A Sitting Ghost," she thought. She pushed against the creature to lever herself out from underneath it, but it absorbed this energy and got heavier. Her fingers and palms became damp, shrinking at the ghost's thick short hair like an animal's coat, which slides against warm solidity as human flesh slides against muscles and bones. She grabbed clutches of fur and pulled. She pinched the skin the hair grew out of and gouged into it with her fingernails. She forced her hands to hunt out eyes, furtive somewhere in the hair, but could not find any. She lifted her head to bite but fell back exhausted. The mass thickened.

She could see the knife, which was catching the moonlight, near the lamp. Her arm had become an immensity, though, too burdensome to lift. If she could only move it to the edge of the bed, perhaps it would fall off and reach the knife. As if feeding on her very thoughts, the ghost spread itself over her arm.

A high ringing sound somewhere had grown loud enough so that she heard it, and she understood that it had started humming at the edge of her brain before the ghost appeared. She breathed shallowly, panting as in childbirth, and could not shout out. The room sang, its air electric with the ringing; surely someone would hear and come help.

Earlier in the night, on the other side of the ringing, she could hear women's voices talking. But soon their conversations had ceased. The school slept. She could feel that the souls had gone travelling; there was a lightness not in the dormitory during the day. Without looking at the babies on her back or in their cribs, she had always been able to tell—after the rocking and singing and bedtime stories and keeping still not to startle them—the moment when they fell asleep. A tensing goes out of their bodies, out of the house. Beyond the horror in the ghost room, she felt this release throughout the dormitory. No one would come to see how she was doing.

"You will not win, Boulder," she spoke to the ghost. "You do not belong here. And I will see to it that you leave. When morning comes, only one of us will control this room, Ghost, and that one will be me. I will be marching its length and width; I will be dancing, not sliding and creeping like you. I will go right out that door, but I'll come back. Do you know what gift I will bring you? I'll get fire, Ghost. You made a mistake haunting a medical school. We have cabinets full of alcohol, laboratories full. We have a communal kitchen with human-sized jars of oil and cooking fat, enough to burn for a month without our skipping a single fried meal. I will pour alcohol into my washbucket, and I'll set fire to it. Ghost, I will burn you out. I will swing the bucket across the ceiling. Then from the kitchen my friends will come with the lard; when we fire it, the smoke will fill every crack and corner. Where will you hide, Ghost? I will make this room so clean, no ghost will ever visit here again.

"I do not give in," she said. "There is no pain you can inflict that I cannot endure. You're wrong if you think I'm afraid of you. You're no mystery to me. I've heard of you Sitting Ghosts before. Yes, people have lived to tell about you. You kill babies, you cowards. You have no power over a strong woman. You are no more dangerous than a nesting cat. My dog sits on my feet more heavily than you can. You think this is suffering? I can make my ears ring louder by taking aspirin. Are these all the tricks you have, Ghost? Sitting and ringing? That is nothing. A Broom Ghost can do better. You cannot even assume an interesting shape. Merely a boulder. A hairy butt boulder. You must not be a ghost at all. Of course. There are no such things as ghosts.

"Let me instruct you, Boulder. When Yen, the teacher, was grading the provincial exams one year, a thing with hair as ugly as yours plopped itself on his desk. (That one had glaring eyes, though, so it wasn't blind and stupid like you.) Yen picked up his ferule and hit it like a student. He chased it around the room. (It wasn't lame and lazy.) And it vanished. Later Yen taught us, 'After life, the rational soul ascends the dragon; the sentient soul descends the dragon. So in the world there can be no ghosts. This thing must have been a Fox Spirit.' That must be just what you are—a Fox Spirit. You are so hairy, you must be a fox that doesn't even know how to transform itself. You're not clever for a Fox Spirit, I must say. No tricks. No blood. Where are your hanged man's rotting noose and icy breath? No throwing shoes into the rafters? No metamorphosis into a beautiful sad lady? No disguises in my dead relatives' shapes? No drowned woman with seaweed hair? No riddles or penalty games? You are a puny little boulder indeed. Yes, when I get my oil, I will fry you for breakfast."

She then ignored the ghost on her chest and chanted her lessons for the next day's classes. The moon moved from one window to the other, and as dawn came, the thing scurried off, climbing quickly down the foot of the bed.

She fell asleep until time for school. She had said she was going to sleep in that room, and so she did.

She awoke when the students came tumbling into the room. "What happened?" they asked, getting under the quilt to keep warm. "Did anything happen?"

"Take my earlobes, please," said my mother, "and pull them back and forth. In case I lost any of my self, I want you to call me back. I was afraid, and fear may have driven me out of my body and mind. Then I will tell you the story." Two friends clasped her hands while a third held her head and took each earlobe between thumb and forefinger, wiggling them and chanting, "Come home, come home, Brave Orchid, who has fought the ghosts and won. Return to To Keung School, Kwangtung City, Kwangtung Province. Your classmates are here waiting for you, scholarly Brave Orchid. Come home. Come home. Come back and help us with our lessons. School is starting soon. Come for breakfast. Return, daughter of New Society Village, Kwangtung Province. Your brother and sisters call you. Your friends call you. We need you. Return to us. Return to us at the To Keung School. There's work to do. Come back, Doctor Brave Orchid, be unafraid. Be unafraid. You are safe now in the To Keung School. All is safe. Return."

Abundant comfort in long restoring waves warmed my mother. Her soul returned fully to her and nestled happily inside her skin, for this moment not travelling in the past where her children were nor to America to be with my father. She was back among many people. She rested after battle. She let friends watch out for her.

"There," said the roommate, giving her ear a last hearty tug, "you are cured. Now tell us what happened."

"I had finished reading my novel," said my mother, "and still nothing happened. I was listening to the dogs bark far away. Suddenly a full-grown Sitting Ghost loomed up to the ceiling and pounced on top of me. Mounds of hair hid its claws and teeth. No true head, no eyes, no face, so low in its level of incarnation it did not have the shape of a recognizable animal. It knocked me down and began to strangle me. It was bigger than a wolf, bigger than an ape, and growing. I would have stabbed it. I would have cut it up, and we would be mopping blood this morning, but—a Sitting Ghost mutation—it had an extra arm that wrested my hand away from the knife.

"At about 3 A.M. I died for a while. I was wandering, and the world I touched turned into sand. I could hear wind, but the sand did not fly. For ten years I lost my way. I almost forgot about you; there was so much work leading to other work and another life—like picking up coins in a dream. But I returned. I walked from the Gobi Desert to this room in the To Keung School. That took another two years, outwitting Wall Ghosts en route. (The way to do that is to go straight ahead; do not play their side-to-side games. In confusion they will instantly revert to their real state—weak and sad humanity. No matter what, don't commit suicide, or you will have to trade places with the Wall Ghost. If you are not put off by the foot-long lolling tongues and the popped-out eyes of the hanged ones or the open

veins or the drowned skin and seaweed hair—and you
shouldn't be because you're doctors—you can chant these
poor souls on to light.)

"No white bats and no black bats flew ahead to guide me
to my natural death. Either I would die without my whole
life or I would not die. I did not die. I am brave and good.
Also I have bodily strength and control. Good people do not
lose to ghosts.

"Altogether I was gone for twelve years, but in this
room only an hour had passed. The moon barely moved. By
silver light I saw the black thing pulling shadows into itself,
setting up magnetic whorls. Soon it would suck in the room
and begin on the rest of the dormitory. It would eat us up.
It threw boulders at me. And there was a sound like mountain wind, a sound so high it could drive you crazy. Didn't
you hear it?"

Yes, they had. Wasn't it like the electric wires that one
sometimes heard in the city? Yes, it was the sound of
energy amassing.

"You were lucky you slept because the sound tears the
heart. I could hear babies crying in it. I could hear tortured
people screaming, and the cries of their relatives who had to
watch."

"Yes, yes, I recognize that. That must have been the
singing I heard in my dream."

"It may be sounding even now, though too strangely for
our daytime ears. You cannot hit the ghost if you sweep
under the bed. The ghost fattens at night, its dark sacs
empty by daylight. It's a good thing I stopped it feeding on
me; blood and meat would have given it strength to feed
on you. I made my will an eggshell encasing the monster's
fur so that the hollow hairs could not draw. I never let up
willing its size smaller, its hairs to retract, until by dawn
the Sitting Ghost temporarily disappeared.

"The danger is not over. The ghost is listening to us
right now, and tonight it will walk again but stronger. We
may not be able to control it if you do not help me finish it

off before sundown. This Sitting Ghost has many wide black mouths. It is dangerous. It is real. Most ghosts make such brief and gauzy appearances that eyewitnesses doubt their own sightings. This one can conjure up enough substance to sit solidly throughout a night. It is a serious ghost, not at all playful. It does not twirl incense sticks or throw shoes and dishes. It does not play peekaboo or wear fright masks. It does not bother with tricks. It wants lives. I am sure it is surfeited with babies and is now coming after adults. It grows. It is mysterious, not merely a copy of ourselves as, after all, the hanged men and seaweed women are. It could be hiding right now in a piece of wood or inside one of your dolls. Perhaps in daylight we accept that bag to be just a bag"—she pointed with the flat of her palm as if it balanced a top—"when in reality it is a Bag Ghost." The students moved away from the bag in which they collected their quilting scraps and pulled up their feet that were dangling over the edge of the bed.

"You have to help me rid the world of this disease, as invisible and deadly as bacteria. After classes, come back here with your buckets, alcohol, and oil. If you can find dog's blood too, our work will go fast. Act unafraid. Ghost chasers have to be brave. If the ghost comes after you, though I would not expect an attack during the day, spit at it. Scorn it. The hero in a ghost story laughs a nimble laugh, his life so full it splatters red and gold on all the creatures around him."

These young women, who would have to back up their science with magical spells should their patients be disappointed and not get well, now hurried to get to classes on time. The story about the ghost's appearance and the coming ghost chase grew, and students snatched alcohol and matches from the laboratories.

My mother directed the arrangement of the buckets and burners into orderly rows and divided the fuel. "Let's fire the oil all at once," she said. "Now."

"Whup. Whup." My mother told the sound of new fire so that I remember it. "Whup. Whup."

The alcohol burned a floating blue. The tarry oil, which someone had bought from her village witch, fumed in black clouds. My mother swung a big bucket overhead. The smoke curled in black boas around the women in their scholars' black gowns. They walked the ghost room, this circle of little black women, lifting smoke and fire up to the ceiling corners, down to the floor corners, moving clouds across the walls and floors, under the bed, around one another.

"I told you, Ghost," my mother chanted, "that we would come after you." "We told you, Ghost, that we would come after you," sang the women. "Daylight has come yellow and red," sang my mother, "and we are winning. Run, Ghost, run from this school. Only good medical people belong here. Go back, dark creature, to your native country. Go home. Go home." "Go home," sang the women.

When the smoke cleared, I think my mother said that under the foot of the bed the students found a piece of wood dripping with blood. They burned it in one of the pots, and the stench was like a corpse exhumed for its bones too soon. They laughed at the smell.

The students at the To Keung School of Midwifery were new women, scientists who changed the rituals. When she got scared as a child, one of my mother's three mothers had held her and chanted their descent line, reeling the frighted spirit back from the farthest deserts. A relative would know personal names and secrets about husbands, babies, renegades and decide which ones were lucky in a chant, but these outside women had to build a path from scraps. No blood bonded friend to friend (though there were things owed beggars and monks), and they had to figure out how to help my mother's spirit locate the To Keung School as "home." The calling out of her real descent line would have led her to the wrong place, the village. These strangers had to make her come back to them. They called out their own names, women's pretty names, haphazard names, horizontal names of one generation. They pieced together new directions, and my mother's spirit followed them instead of the old footprints. Maybe that is why she lost her home village and did not reach her husband for fifteen years.

When my mother led us out of nightmares and horror movies, I felt loved. I felt safe hearing my name sung with hers and my father's, my brothers' and sisters', her anger at children who hurt themselves surprisingly gone. An old-fashioned woman would have called in the streets for her sick child. She'd hold its little empty coat unbuttoned, "Come put on your coat, you naughty child." When the coat puffed up, she'd quickly button up the spirit inside and hurry it home to the child's body in bed. But my mother, a modern woman, said our spells in private. "The old ladies in China had many silly superstitions," she said. "I know you'll come back without my making a fool of myself in the streets."

Not when we were afraid, but when we were wide awake and lucid, my mother funneled China into our ears: Kwangtung Province, New Society Village, the river Kwoo, which runs past the village. "Go the way we came so that you will be able to find our house. Don't forget. Just give your father's name, and any villager can point out our house." I am to return to China where I have never been.

After two years of study—the graduates of three-week and six-week courses were more admired by the peasants for learning at such wondrous speeds—my mother returned to her home village a doctor. She was welcomed with garlands and cymbals the way people welcome the "barefoot doctors" today. But the Communists wear a blue plainness dotted with one red Mao button. My mother wore a silk robe and western shoes with big heels, and she rode home carried in a sedan chair. She had gone away ordinary and come back miraculous, like the ancient magicians who came down from the mountains.

"When I stepped out of my sedan chair, the villagers

said, 'Ahhh,' at my good shoes and my long gown. I always dressed well when I made calls. Some villages brought out their lion and danced ahead of me. You have no idea how much I have fallen coming to America." Until my father sent for her to live in the Bronx, my mother delivered babies in beds and pigsties. She stayed awake keeping watch nightly in an epidemic and chanted during air raids. She yanked bones straight that had been crooked for years while relatives held the cripples down, and she did all this never dressed less elegantly than when she stepped out of the sedan chair.

Nor did she change her name: Brave Orchid. Professional women have the right to use their maiden names if they like. Even when she emigrated, my mother kept Brave Orchid, adding no American name nor holding one in reserve for American emergencies.

Walking behind the palanquin so that the crowd took her for one of themselves following the new doctor came a quiet girl. She carried a white puppy and a rice sack knotted at the mouth. Her pigtails and the puppy's tail ended in red yarn. She may have been either a daughter or a slave.

When my mother had gone to Canton market to shop, her wallet had unfolded like wings. She had received her diploma, and it was time to celebrate. She had hunted out the seed shops to taste their lichees, various as wines, and bought a sack that was taller than a child to bedazzle the nieces and nephews. A merchant had given her one nut fresh on its sprig of narrow leaves. My mother popped the thin wood shell in her curled palm. The white fruit, an eye without an iris, ran juices like spring rivers inside my mother's mouth. She spit out the brown seed, iris after all.

She had bought a turtle for my grandfather because it would lengthen his life. She had dug to the bottom of fabric piles and explored the shadows underneath awnings. She gave beggars rice and letter-writers coins so that they would talk-story. ("Sometimes what I gave was all they had, and stories.") She let a fortuneteller read the whorls on her fingerprints; he predicted that she would leave China and have six more children. "Six," he said, "is the number of everything. You are such a lucky woman. Six is the universe's number. The four compass points plus the zenith and the nadir are six. There are six low phoenix notes and six high, six worldly environments, six senses, six virtues, six obligations, six classes of ideograph, six domestic animals, six arts, and six paths of metempsychosis. More than two thousand years ago, six states combined to overthrow Ch'in. And, of course, there are the hexagrams that are the *I Ching*, and there is the Big Six, which is China." As interesting as his list of sixes was, my mother hurried on her way; she had come to market to buy herself a slave.

Between the booths and stores, whoever could squeeze a space—a magician who could turn dirt into gold, twenty-five acrobats on one unicycle, a man who could swim—displayed his or her newest feat for money. From the country the villagers brought strange purple textiles, dolls with big feet, geese with brown tufts on their heads, chickens with white feathers and black skin, gambling games and puppet shows, intricate ways to fold pastry and ancestors' money, a new boxing stance.

Herders roped off alleys to pen their goats, which stared out of the dimness with rectangular pupils. Whisking a handful of grass, my mother coaxed them into the light and watched the tiny yellow windows close and open again as the goats skipped backward into the shade. Two farmers, each leading this year's cow, passed each other, shouting prices. Usually my mother would have given herself up to the pleasure of being in a crowd, delighting in the money game the people would play with the rival herders, who were now describing each other's cows—"skinny shoulder blades," "lame legs," "patchy hair," "ogre face." But today she hurried even when looking over the monkey cages stacked higher than her head. She paused only a while in front of the ducks, which honked madly, the down flying as some passer-by bumped into their cages. My mother liked to look at the ducks and plan how she would dig a pond for them near the sweet potato field and arrange straw for their eggs. She decided that the drake with the green head would be the best buy, the noblest, although she would not buy him unless she had money left over; she was already raising a nobler duck on the farm.

Among the sellers with their ropes, cages, and water tanks were the sellers of little girls. Sometimes just one man would be standing by the side of the road selling one girl. There were fathers and mothers selling their daughters, whom they pushed forward and then pulled back again. My mother turned her face to look at pottery or embroidery rather than at these miserable families who did not have the sense to leave the favored brothers and sisters home. All the children bore still faces. My mother would not buy from parents, crying and clutching. They would try to keep you talking to find out what kind of mistress you were to your slaves. If they could just hear from the buyer's own mouth about a chair in the kitchen, they could tell each other in the years to come that their daughter was even now resting in the kitchen chair. It was merciful to give these parents a few details about the garden, a sweet feeble grandmother, food.

My mother would buy her slave from a professional whose little girls stood neatly in a row and bowed together when a customer looked them over. "How do you do, Sir?" they would sing. "How do you do, Madam?" "Let a little slave do your shopping for you," the older girls chorused. "We've been taught to bargain. We've been taught to sew. We can cook, and we can knit." Some of the dealers merely had the children bow quietly. Others had them sing a happy song about flowers.

Unless a group of little girls chanted some especially clever riddle, my mother, who distrusts people with public concerns, braggarts, went over to the quiet older girls with the dignified bows. "Any merchant who advertises 'Honest

Scales' must have been thinking about weighting them," she says. Many sellers displayed the sign "Children and Old Men Not Cheated."

There were girls barely able to toddle carrying infant slaves tied in slings to their backs. In the undisciplined groups the babies crawled into gutters and the older girls each acted as if she were alone, a daughter among slaves. The one- to two-year-old babies cost nothing.

"Greet the lady," the dealer commanded, just as the nice little girls' mothers had when visitors came.

"How do you do, Lady," said the girls.

My mother did not need to bow back, and she did not. She overlooked the infants and toddlers and talked to the oldest girls.

"Open your mouth," she said, and examined teeth. She pulled down eyelids to check for anemia. She picked up the girls' wrists to sound their pulses, which tell everything.

She stopped at a girl whose strong heart sounded like thunder within the earth, sending its power into her fingertips. "I would not have sold a daughter such as that one," she told us. My mother could find no flaw in the beat; it matched her own, the real rhythm. There were people jumpy with silly rhythms; broken rhythms; sly, secretive rhythms. They did not follow the sounds of earth-sea-sky and the Chinese language.

My mother brought out the green notebook my father had given her when he left. It had a map of each hemisphere on the inside covers and a clasp that shut it like a pocketbook. "Watch carefully," she said. With an American pencil, she wrote a word, a felicitous word such as "longevity" or "double joy," which is symmetrical.

"Look carefully," she said into the girl's face. "If you can write this word from memory, I will take you with me. Concentrate now." She wrote in a plain style and folded the page a moment afterward. The girl took the pencil and wrote surely; she did not leave out a single stroke.

"What would you do," my mother asked, "if you lost a gold watch in a field?"

"I know a chant on the finger bones," said the girl. "But even if I landed on the bone that says to look no more, I would go to the middle of the field and search in a spiral going outward until I reached the field's edge. Then I would believe the chant and look no more." She drew in my mother's notebook the field and her spiraling path.

"How do you cast on yarn?"

The girl pantomimed her method with her large hands.

"How much water do you put in the rice pot for a family of five? How do you finish off weaving so that it doesn't unravel?"

Now it was time to act as if she were very dissatisfied with the slave's answers so that the dealer would not charge her extra for a skillful worker.

"You tie the loose ends into tassles," said the girl.

My mother frowned. "But suppose I like a finished border?"

The girl hesitated. "I could, uh, press the fibers under and sew them down. Or how about cutting the fibers off?"

My mother offered the dealer half the price he named. "My mother-in-law asked me to find a weaver for her, and obviously she and I will have to waste many months training this girl."

"But she can knit and cook," said the dealer, "and she can find lost watches." He asked for a price higher than her suggestion but lower than his first.

"I knit and cook and find things," said my mother. "How else do you suppose I think of such ingenious questions? Do you think I would buy a slave who could outwork me in front of my mother-in-law?" My mother walked off to look at a group of hungry slaves across the street. When she returned, the dealer sold her the girl with the finding chant at my mother's price.

"I am a doctor," she told her new slave, when they were out of the dealer's hearing, "and I shall train you to be my nurse."

"Doctor," said the slave, "do you understand that I do know how to finish off my weaving?"

"Yes, we fooled him very well," said my mother.

The unsold slaves must have watched them with envy. I watch them with envy. My mother's enthusiasm for me is duller than for the slave girl; nor did I replace the older brother and sister who died while they were still cuddly. Throughout childhood my younger sister said, "When I grow up, I want to be a slave," and my parents laughed, encouraging her. At department stores I angered my mother when I could not bargain without shame, poor people's shame. She stood in back of me and prodded and pinched, forcing me to translate her bargaining, word for word.

On that same day she bought at the dog dealer's a white puppy to train as her bodyguard when she made night calls. She tied pretty red yarn around its tail to neutralize the bad luck. There was no use docking the tail. No matter at what point she cut, the tip would have been white, the mourning color.

The puppy waved its red yarn at the nurse girl, and she picked it up. She followed my mother back to the village, where she always got enough to eat because my mother became a good doctor. She could cure the most spectacular diseases. When a sick person was about to die, my mother could read the fact of it a year ahead of time on the daughters-in-law's faces. A black veil seemed to hover over their skin. And though they laughed, this blackness rose and fell with their breath. My mother would take one look at the daughter-in-law who answered the door at the sick house and she'd say, "Find another doctor." She would not touch death; therefore, untainted, she brought only health from house to house. "She must be a Jesus convert," the people from the far villages said. "All her patients get well." The bigger the talk, the farther the distances she travelled. She had customers everywhere.

Sometimes she went to her patients by foot. Her nurse-slave carried an umbrella when my mother predicted rain and a parasol when she predicted sun. "My white dog would be standing at the door waiting for me whenever I came home," she said. When she felt like it, my mother would leave the nurse-slave to watch the office and would take the white dog with her.

"What happened to your dog when you came to America, Mother?"

"I don't know."

"What happened to the slave?"

"I found her a husband."

"How much money did you pay to buy her?"

"One hundred and eighty dollars."

"How much money did you pay the doctor and the hospital when I was born?"

"Two hundred dollars."

"Oh."

"That's two hundred dollars American money."

"Was the one hundred and eighty dollars American money?"

"No."

"How much was it American money?"

"Fifty dollars. That's because she was sixteen years old. Eight-year-olds were about twenty dollars. Five-year-olds were ten dollars and up. Two-year-olds were about five dollars. Babies were free. During the war, though, when you were born, many people gave older girls away for free. And here I was in the United States paying two hundred dollars for you."

When my mother went doctoring in the villages, the ghosts, the were-people, the apes dropped out of trees. They rose out of bridge water. My mother saw them come out of cervixes. Medical science does not seal the earth, whose nether creatures seep out, hair by hair, disguised like the smoke that dispels them. She had apparently won against the one ghost, but ghost forms are various and many. Some can occupy the same space at the same moment. They permeate the grain in wood, metal, and stone. Animalcules somersault about our faces when we breathe. We have to build horns on our roofs so that the nagging once-people can slide up them and perhaps ascend to the stars, the source of pardon and love.

On a fine spring day the villagers at a place my mother had never visited before would wave peach branches and fans, which are emblems of Chung-li Ch'uan, the chief of the Eight Sages and keeper of the elixir of life. The pink petals would fall on my mother's black hair and gown. The villagers would set off firecrackers as on New Year's Day. If it had really been New Year's, she would have had to shut herself up in her own house. Nobody wanted a doctor's visit in the first days of the year.

But at night my mother walked quickly. She and bandits were the only human beings out, no palanquins available for midwives. For a time the roads were endangered by a fantastic creature, half man and half ape, that a traveller to the West had captured and brought back to China in a cage. With his new money, the man had built the fourth wing to his house, and in the courtyard he grew a stand of bamboo. The ape-man could reach out and touch the thin leaves that shaded its cage.

This creature had gnawed through the bars. Or it had tricked its owner into letting it play in the courtyard, and then leapt over the roof of the new wing. Now it was at large in the forests, living off squirrels, mice, and an occasional duck or piglet. My mother saw in the dark a denser dark, and she knew she was being followed. She carried a club, and the white dog was beside her. The ape-man was known to have attacked people. She had treated their bites and claw wounds. With hardly a rustle of leaves, the ape-man leapt live out of the trees and blocked her way. The white dog yelped. As big as a human being, the ape-thing jumped up and down on one foot. Its two hands were holding the other foot, hurt in the jump. It had long orange hair and beard. Its owner had clothed it in a brown burlap rice sack with holes for neck and arms. It blinked at my mother with human eyes, moving its head from shoulder to shoulder as if figuring things out. "Go home," she shouted, waving her club. It copied her waving with one raised arm and made complex motions with its other hand. But when she rushed at it, it turned and ran limping into the forest. "Don't you scare me again," she yelled after its retreating buttocks, tailless and hairless under the shirt. It was definitely not a gorilla; she has since seen some of those at the Bronx Zoo, and this ape-man was nothing like them. If her father had not brought Third Wife, who was not Chinese, back from his travels, my mother might have thought this orange creature with the great nose was a barbarian from the West. But my grandfather's Third Wife was black with hair so soft that it would not hang, instead blowing up into a great brown puffball. (At first she talked constantly, but who could understand her? After a while she never talked anymore. She had one son.) The owner of the ape-man finally recaptured it by luring it back into its cage with cooked pork and wine. Occasionally my mother went to the rich man's house to look at the ape-man. It seemed to recognize her and smiled when she gave it candy. Perhaps it had not been an ape-man at all, but one of the Tigermen, a savage northern race.

My mother was midwife to whatever spewed forth, not being able to choose as with the old and sick. She was not squeamish, though, and deftly caught spewings that were sometimes babies, sometimes monsters. When she helped the country women who insisted on birthing in the pigpen, she could not tell by starlight and moonlight what manner of creature had made its arrival on the earth until she carried it inside the house. "Pretty pigbaby, pretty piglet," she and the mother would croon, fooling the ghosts on the lookout for a new birth. "Ugly pig, dirty pig," fooling the gods jealous of human joy. They counted fingers and toes by touch, felt for penis or no penis, but not until later would they know for sure whether the gods let them get away with something good.

One boy appeared perfect, so round in the cool opal dawn. But when my mother examined him indoors, he opened up blue eyes at her. Perhaps he had looked without protection at the sky, and it had filled him. His mother said that a ghost had entered him, but my mother said the baby looked pretty.

Not all defects could be explained so congenially. One child born without an anus was left in the outhouse so that the family would not have to hear it cry. They kept going back to see whether it was dead yet, but it lived for a long time. Whenever they went to look at it, it was sobbing, heaving as if it were trying to defecate. For days the family either walked to the fields or used the night soil buckets.

As a child, I pictured a naked child sitting on a modern toilet desperately trying to perform until it died of congestion. I had to flick on the bathroom lights fast so that no small shadow would take a baby shape, sometimes seated on the edge of the bathtub, its hopes for a bowel movement so exaggerated. When I woke at night I sometimes heard an infant's grunting and weeping coming from the bathroom. I did not go to its rescue but waited for it to stop.

I hope this holeless baby proves that my mother did not prepare a box of clean ashes beside the birth bed in case of a girl. "The midwife or a relative would take the back of a girl baby's head in her hand and turn her face into the ashes," said my mother. "It was very easy." She never said she herself killed babies, but perhaps the holeless baby was a boy.

Even here on Gold Mountain grateful couples bring gifts to my mother, who had cooked them a soup that not only ended their infertility but gave them a boy.

My mother has given me pictures to dream—nightmare babies that recur, shrinking again and again to fit in my palm. I curl my fingers to make a cradle for the baby, my other hand an awning. I would protect the dream baby, not let it suffer, not let it out of my sight. But in a blink of inattention, I would mislay the baby. I would have to stop moving, afraid of stepping on it. Or before my very eyes, it slips between my fingers because my fingers cannot grow webs fast enough. Or bathing it, I carefully turn the right-hand faucet, but it spouts hot water, scalding the baby until its skin tautens and its face becomes nothing but a red hole of a scream. The hole turns into a pinprick as the baby recedes from me.

To make my waking life American-normal, I turn on the lights before anything untoward makes an appearance. I push the deformed into my dreams, which are in Chinese, the language of impossible stories. Before we can leave our parents, they stuff our heads like the suitcases which they jam-pack with homemade underwear.

When the thermometer in our laundry reached one hundred and eleven degrees on summer afternoons, either my mother or my father would say that it was time to tell another ghost story so that we could get some good chills up our backs. My parents, my brothers, sisters, great-uncle, and "Third Aunt," who wasn't really our aunt but a fellow villager, someone else's third aunt, kept the presses crashing and hissing and shouted out the stories. Those were our successful days, when so much laundry came in, my mother did not have to pick tomatoes. For breaks we changed from pressing to sorting.

"One twilight," my mother began, and already the chills travelled my back and crossed my shoulders; the hair rose at the nape and the back of the legs, "I was walking home after doctoring a sick family. To get home I had to cross a footbridge. In China the bridges are nothing like the ones in Brooklyn and San Francisco. This one was made from rope, laced and knotted as if by magpies. Actually it had been built by men who had returned after harvesting sea swallow nests in Malaya. They had had to swing over the faces of the Malayan cliffs in baskets they had woven them-selves. Though this bridge pitched and swayed in the up-draft, no one had ever fallen into the river, which looked like a bright scratch at the bottom of the canyon, as if the Queen of Heaven had swept her great silver hairpin across the earth as well as the sky."

One twilight, just as my mother stepped on the bridge, two smoky columns spiraled up taller than she. Their swaying tops hovered over her head like white cobras, one at either handrail. From stillness came a wind rushing between the smoke spindles. A high sound entered her temple bones. Through the twin whirlwinds she could see the sun and the river, the river twisting in circles, the trees upside down. The bridge moved like a ship, sickening. The earth dipped. She collapsed to the wooden slats, a ladder up the sky, her fingers so weak she could not grip the rungs. The wind dragged her hair behind her, then whipped it forward across her face. Suddenly the smoke spindles disappeared. The world righted itself, and she crossed to the other side. She looked back, but there was nothing there. She used the bridge often, but she did not encounter those ghosts again.

"They were Sit Dom Kuei," said Great-Uncle. "Sit Dom Kuei."

"Yes, of course," said my mother. "Sit Dom Kuei."

I keep looking in dictionaries under those syllables. "Kuei" means "ghost," but I don't find any other words that make sense. I only hear my great-uncle's river-pirate voice, the voice of a big man who had killed someone in New York or Cuba, make the sounds—"Sit Dom Kuei." How do they translate?

When the Communists issued their papers on techniques for combating ghosts, I looked for "Sit Dom Kuei." I have not found them described anywhere, although now I see that my mother won in ghost battle because she can eat anything—quick, pluck out the carp's eyes, one for Mother and one for Father. All heroes are bold toward food. In the research against ghost fear published by the Chinese Academy of Science is the story of a magistrate's servant, Kao Chung, a capable eater who in 1683 ate five cooked chickens and drank ten bottles of wine that belonged to the sea monster with branching teeth. The monster had arranged its food around a fire on the beach and started to feed when Kao Chung attacked. The swan-feather sword he wrested from this monster can be seen in the Wentung County Armory in Shantung today.

Another big eater was Chou Yi-han of Changchow, who fried a ghost. It was a meaty stick when he cut it up and cooked it. But before that it had been a woman out at night.

Chen Luan-feng, during the Yuan Ho era of the T'ang dynasty (A.D. 806–820), ate yellow croaker and pork together, which the thunder god had forbidden. But Chen wanted to incur thunderbolts during drought. The first time he ate, the thunder god jumped out of the sky, its legs like old trees. Chen chopped off the left one. The thunder god fell to the earth, and the villagers could see that it was a blue pig or bear with horns and fleshy wings. Chen leapt on it, prepared to chop its neck and bite its throat, but the villagers stopped him. After that, Chen lived apart as a rainmaker, neither relatives nor the monks willing to bring lightning upon themselves. He lived in a cave, and for years whenever there was drought the villagers asked him to eat yellow croaker and pork together, and he did.

The most fantastic eater of them all was Wei Pang, a scholar-hunter of the Ta Li era of the T'ang dynasty (A.D. 766–779). He shot and cooked rabbits and birds, but he could also eat scorpions, snakes, cockroaches, worms, slugs, beetles, and crickets. Once he spent the night in a house that had been abandoned because its inhabitants feared contamination from the dead man next door. A shining, twinkling sphere came flying through the darkness at Wei. He felled it with three true arrows—the first making the thing crackle and flame; the second dimming it; and the third putting out its lights, sputter. When his servant came running in with a lamp, Wei saw his arrows sticking in a ball of flesh entirely covered with eyes, some rolled back to show the dulling whites. He and the servant pulled out the arrows and cut up the ball into little pieces. The servant cooked the morsels in sesame oil, and the wonderful aroma made Wei laugh. They ate half, saving half to show the household, which would return now.

Big eaters win. When other passers-by stepped around the bundle wrapped in white silk, the anonymous scholar of Hanchow took it home. Inside were three silver ingots and a froglike evil, which sat on the ingots. The scholar laughed at it and chased it off. That night two frogs the size of year-old babies appeared in his room. He clubbed them to death, cooked them, and ate them with white wine. The next night a dozen frogs, together the size of a pair of year-old babies, jumped from the ceiling. He ate all twelve for dinner. The third night thirty small frogs were sitting on his mat and staring at him with their frog eyes. He ate them too. Every night for a month smaller but more numerous frogs came so that he always had the same amount to eat. Soon his floor was like the healthy banks of a pond in spring when the tadpoles, having just turned, sprang in the wet grass. "Get a hedgehog to help eat," cried his family. "I'm as good as a hedgehog," the scholar said, laughing. And at the end of the month the frogs stopped coming, leaving the scholar with the white silk and silver ingots.

My mother has cooked for us: raccoons, skunks, hawks, city pigeons, wild ducks, wild geese, black-skinned bantams, snakes, garden snails, turtles that crawled about the pantry floor and sometimes escaped under refrigerator or stove, catfish that swam in the bathtub. "The emperors used to eat the peaked hump of purple dromedaries," she would say. "They used chopsticks made from rhinoceros horn, and they ate ducks' tongues and monkeys' lips." She boiled the weeds we pulled up in the yard. There was a tender plant with flowers like white stars hiding under the leaves, which were like the flower petals but green. I've not been able to find it since growing up. It had no taste. When I was as tall as the washing machine, I stepped out on the back porch one night, and some heavy, ruffling, windy, clawed thing dived at me. Even after getting chanted back to sensibility, I shook when I recalled that perched everywhere there were owls with great hunched shoulders and yellow scowls. They were a surprise for my mother from my father. We children used to hide under the beds with our fingers in our ears to shut out the bird screams and the thud, thud of the turtles swimming in the boiling water, their shells hitting the sides of the pot. Once the third aunt who worked at the laundry ran out and bought us bags of candy to hold over our noses; my mother was dismembering skunk on the chopping block. I could smell the rubbery odor through the candy.

In a glass jar on a shelf my mother kept a big brown hand with pointed claws stewing in alcohol and herbs. She must have brought it from China because I do not remember a time when I did not have the hand to look at. She said it was a bear's claw, and for many years I thought bears were hairless. My mother used the tobacco, leeks, and grasses swimming about the hand to rub our sprains and bruises.

Just as I would climb up to the shelf to take one look after another at the hand, I would hear my mother's monkey story. I'd take my fingers out of my ears and let her monkey words enter my brain. I did not always listen voluntarily, though. She would begin telling the story, perhaps repeating it to a homesick villager, and I'd overhear before I had a chance to protect myself. Then the monkey words would unsettle me; a curtain flapped loose inside my brain. I have wanted to say, "Stop it. Stop it," but not once did I say, "Stop it."

"Do you know what people in China eat when they have the money?" my mother began. "They buy into a monkey feast. The eaters sit around a thick wood table with a hole in the middle. Boys bring in the monkey at the end of a pole. Its neck is in a collar at the end of the pole, and it is screaming. Its hands are tied behind it. They clamp the monkey into the table; the whole table fits like another collar around its neck. Using a surgeon's saw, the cooks cut a clean line in a circle at the top of its head. To loosen the bone, they tap with a tiny hammer and wedge here and there with a silver pick. Then an old woman reaches out her hand to the monkey's face and up to its scalp, where she tufts some hairs and lifts off the lid of the skull. The eaters spoon out the brains."

Did she say, "You should have seen the faces the monkey made"? Did she say, "The people laughed at the monkey screaming"? It was alive? The curtain flaps closed like merciful black wings.

"Eat! Eat!" my mother would shout at our heads bent over bowls, the blood pudding awobble in the middle of the table.

She had one rule to keep us safe from toadstools and such: "If it tastes good, it's bad for you," she said. "If it tastes bad, it's good for you."

We'd have to face four- and five-day-old leftovers until we ate it all. The squid eye would keep appearing at breakfast and dinner until eaten. Sometimes brown masses sat on every dish. I have seen revulsion on the faces of visitors who've caught us at meals.

"Have you eaten yet?" the Chinese greet one another.

"Yes, I have," they answer whether they have or not. "And you?"

I would live on plastic.

My mother could contend against the hairy beasts whether flesh or ghost because she could eat them, and she could not-eat them on the days when good people fast. My mother was not crazy for seeing ghosts nor was she one of those the women teased for "longing" after men. She was a capable exorcist; she did not "long" ("mong" in Cantonese). The village crazy lady was somebody else, an inappropriate woman whom the people stoned.

It was just after this stoning that my mother left

China. My father had made the money for the fare at last, but he sent for her instead of returning, one more postponement of home, this time because of the Japanese. By 1939 the Japanese had taken much of the land along the Kwoo River, and my mother was living in the mountains with other refugees. (I used to watch my mother and father play refugees, sleeping sitting up, huddled together with their heads on each other's shoulder, their arms about each other, holding up the blanket like a little tent. "Aiaa," they'd sigh. "Aiaa." "Mother, what's a refugee? Father, what's a refugee?") The Japanese, though "little," were not ghosts, the only foreigners considered not ghosts by the Chinese. They may have been descended from the Chinese explorers that the First Emperor of Ch'in (221–210 B.C.) had deployed to find longevity medicine. They were to look for an island beyond the Eastern Ocean, beyond the impassable wind and mist. On this island lived phoenixes, unicorns, black apes, and white stags. Magic orchids, strange trees, and plants of jasper grew on Penglai, a fairy mountain, which may have been Mount Fuji. The emperor would saw off the explorers' heads if they returned without the herbs of immortality. Another ancestor of the Japanese is said to be an ape that raped a Chinese princess, who then fled to the eastern islands to have the first Japanese child. Whichever the case, they were not a totally alien species, connected as they were even to royalty. Chinese without sons stole the boy babies of Japanese settlers who left them bundled up at the ends of the potato rows.

Now the villagers were watching for Japanese airplanes that strafed the mountainsides every day. "If you see a single plane, you needn't be afraid," my mother taught us. "But watch for planes in threes. When they spread apart, you know they're going to drop bombs. Sometimes airplanes covered the sky, and we could not see and we could not hear." She warned us because it was the same war still going on years after she crossed the ocean and had us. I huddled under my blankets when Pan Am and United Air

Lines planes flew overhead, the engines sounding like insects at first and getting louder and louder.

In the mountains my mother set up a hospital in a cave, and she carried the wounded there. Some villagers had never seen an airplane before. Mothers stopped up their babies' mouths so their crying would not attract the planes. The bombing drove people insane. They rolled on the ground, pushed themselves against it, as if the earth could open a door for them. The ones who could not stop shaking after the danger passed would sleep in the cave. My mother explained airplanes to them as she wiggled their ears.

One afternoon peace and summer rested on the mountains. Babies napped in the tall grass, their blankets covering the wildflowers with embroidered flowers. It was so quiet; the bees hummed and the river water played the pebbles, the rocks, and the hollows. Cows under the trees whisked their tails; goats and ducks followed the children here and there; and the chickens scratched in the dirt. The villagers stood about in the sunshine. They smiled at one another. Here they all were together, idle above their fields, nobody hoeing, godlike; nobody weeding, New Year's in summer. My mother and the women her age talked about how similar this day was to the orderly days long ago when they walked up the mountain to collect firewood, only now they could dally without the mothers-in-law scolding.

The village crazy lady put on her headdress with the small mirrors, some of them waving quickly on red stalks. In her crazy lady clothes of reds and greens, she greeted the animals and the moving branches as she carried her porcelain cup to the river. Although her bindings had come loose, her tiny feet made her body sway pleasantly, her shoes like little bridges. She knelt singing at the river and filled her cup. Carrying the brimming water in two careful hands, she undulated toward a clearing where the light of the afternoon seemed to be concentrated. The villagers turned to look at her. She dipped her fingertips into the water and flung droplets into grass and air. Then she set the cup down and pulled out the long white undersleeves of her old-fashioned dress. She began to move in fanning circles, now flying the sleeves in the air, now trailing them on the grass, dancing in the middle of the light. The little mirrors in her headdress shot rainbows into the green, glinted off the water cup, caught water drops. My mother felt as if she were peering into Li T'ieh-kuai's magic gourd to check the fate of an impish mortal.

One villager whispered away the spell, "She's signaling the planes." The whisper carried. "She's signaling the planes," the people repeated. "Stop her. Stop her."

"No, she's only crazy," said my mother. "She's a harmless crazy lady."

"She's a spy. A spy for the Japanese."

Villagers picked up rocks and moved down the hill.

"Just take away the mirrors," my mother called. "Just take her headdress."

But the tentative first stones were already falling around the crazy lady. She dodged them; she tried to catch them, laughing, at last, people to play with.

The rocks hit harder as the villagers came within stoning range. "Here. Here. I'll get her mirrors," said my mother, who had come running down the mountain into the clearing. "Give me your headdress," she ordered, but the woman only shook her head coquettishly.

"See? She's a spy. Get out of the way, Doctor. You saw the way she flashed the signals. She comes to the river every day before the planes come."

"She's only getting drinking water," said my mother. "Crazy people drink water too."

Someone took the crazy lady's cup and threw it at her. It broke at her feet. "Are you a spy? Are you?" they asked her.

A cunning look narrowed her eyes. "Yes," she said, "I have great powers. I can make the sky rain fire. Me. I did that. Leave me alone or I will do it again." She edged toward the river as if she were about to run, but she wouldn't have been able to get away on her tiny feet.

A large stone rammed her head, and she fell in a flutter

of sleeves, the ornaments jumping about her broken head. The villagers closed in. Somebody held a fragment of glass under her nostrils. When it clouded, they pounded her temples with the rocks in their fists until she was dead. Some villagers remained at the body beating her head and face, smashing the little mirrors into silver splinters.

My mother, who had turned her back and walked up the mountain (she never treated those about to die), looked down at the mass of flesh and rocks, the sleeves, the blood flecks. The planes came again that very afternoon. The villagers buried the crazy lady along with the rest of the dead.

My mother left China in the winter of 1939, almost six months after the stoning, and arrived in New York Harbor in January, 1940. She carried the same suitcase she had taken to Canton, this time filled with seeds and bulbs. On Ellis Island the officials asked her, "What year did your husband cut off his pigtail?" and it terrified her when she could not remember. But later she told us perhaps this lapse was for the best: what if they were trying to trap him politically? The men had cut their pigtails to defy the Manchus and to help Sun Yat-sen, fellow Cantonese.

I was born in the middle of World War II. From earliest awareness, my mother's stories always timely, I watched for three airplanes parting. Much as I dream recurringly about shrinking babies, I dream that the sky is covered from horizon to horizon with rows of airplanes, dirigibles, rocket ships, flying bombs, their formations as even as stitches. When the sky seems clear in my dreams and I would fly, if I look too closely, there so silent, far away, and faint in the daylight that people who do not know about them do not see them, are shiny silver machines, some not yet invented, being moved, fleets always being moved from one continent to another, one planet to another. I must figure out a way to fly between them.

But America has been full of machines and ghosts—

Taxi Ghosts, Bus Ghosts, Police Ghosts, Fire Ghosts, Meter Reader Ghosts, Tree Trimming Ghosts, Five-and-Dime Ghosts. Once upon a time the world was so thick with ghosts, I could hardly breathe; I could hardly walk, limping my way around the White Ghosts and their cars. There were Black Ghosts too, but they were open eyed and full of laughter, more distinct than White Ghosts.

What frightened me most was the Newsboy Ghost, who came out from between the cars parked in the evening light. Carrying a newspaper pouch instead of a baby brother, he walked right out in the middle of the street without his parents. He shouted ghost words to the empty streets. His voice reached children inside the houses, reached inside the children's chests. They would come running out of their yards with their dimes. They would follow him just a corner too far. And when they went to the nearest house to ask directions home, the Gypsy Ghosts would lure them inside with gold rings and then boil them alive and bottle them. The ointment thus made was good for rubbing on children's bruises.

We used to pretend we were Newsboy Ghosts. We collected old Chinese newspapers (the Newsboy Ghost not giving us his ghost newspapers) and trekked about the house and yard. We waved them over our heads, chanting a chant: "Newspapers for sale. Buy a newspaper." But those who could hear the insides of words heard that we were selling a miracle salve made from boiled children. The newspapers covered up green medicine bottles. We made up our own English, which I wrote down and now looks like "eeeeeeeeee." When we heard the real newsboy calling, we hid, dragging our newspapers under the stairs or into the cellar, where the Well Ghost lived in the black water under a lid. We crouched on our newspapers, the San Francisco *Gold Mountain News*, and plugged up our ears with our knuckles until he went away.

For our very food we had to traffic with the Grocery Ghosts, the supermarket aisles full of ghost customers. The

Milk Ghost drove his white truck from house to house every other day. We hid watching until his truck turned the corner, bottles rattling in their frames. Then we unlocked the front door and the screen door and reached for the milk. We were regularly visited by the Mail Ghost, Meter Reader Ghost, Garbage Ghost. Staying off the streets did no good. They came nosing at windows—Social Worker Ghosts; Public Health Nurse Ghosts; Factory Ghosts recruiting workers during the war (they promised free child care, which our mother turned down); two Jesus Ghosts who had formerly worked in China. We hid directly under the windows, pressed against the baseboard until the ghost, calling us in the ghost language so that we'd almost answer to stop its voice, gave up. They did not try to break in, except for a few Burglar Ghosts. The Hobo Ghosts and Wino Ghosts took peaches off our trees and drank from the hose when nobody answered their knocks.

It seemed as if ghosts could not hear or see very well. Momentarily lulled by the useful chores they did for whatever ghostly purpose, we did not bother to lower the windows one morning when the Garbage Ghost came. We talked loudly about him through the fly screen, pointed at his hairy arms, and laughed at how he pulled up his dirty pants before swinging his hoard onto his shoulders. "Come see the Garbage Ghost get its food," we children called. "The Garbage Ghost," we told each other, nodding our heads. The ghost looked directly at us. Steadying the load on his back with one hand, the Garbage Ghost walked up to the window. He had cavernous nostrils with yellow and brown hair. Slowly he opened his red mouth, "The . . . Gar . . . bage . . . Ghost," he said, copying human language. "Gar . . . bage . . . Ghost?" We ran, screaming to our mother, who efficiently shut the window. "Now we know," she told us, "the White Ghosts can hear Chinese. They have learned it. You mustn't talk in front of them again. Someday, very soon, we're going home, where there are Han people everywhere. We'll buy furniture then, real tables and chairs. You children will smell flowers for the first time."

"Mother! Mother! It's happening again. I taste something in my mouth, but I'm not eating anything."

"Me too, Mother. Me too. There's nothing there. Just my spit. My spit tastes like sugar."

"Your grandmother in China is sending you candy again," said my mother. Human beings do not need Mail Ghosts to send messages.

I must have tinkered too much wondering how my invisible grandmother, illiterate and dependent on letter writers, could give us candy free. When I got older and more scientific, I received no more gifts from her. She died, and I did not get "home" to ask her how she did it. Whenever my parents said "home," they suspended America. They suspended enjoyment, but I did not want to go to China. In China my parents would sell my sisters and me. My father would marry two or three more wives, who would spatter cooking oil on our bare toes and lie that we were crying for naughtiness. They would give food to their own children and rocks to us. I did not want to go where the ghosts took shapes nothing like our own.

As a child I feared the size of the world. The farther away the sound of howling dogs, the farther away the sound of the trains, the tighter I curled myself under the quilt. The trains sounded deeper and deeper into the night. They had not reached the end of the world before I stopped hearing them, the last long moan diminishing toward China. How large the world must be to make my grandmother only a taste by the time she reaches me.

When I last visited my parents, I had trouble falling asleep, too big for the hills and valleys scooped in the mattress by child-bodies. I heard my mother come in. I stopped moving. What did she want? Eyes shut, I pictured my mother, her white hair frizzy in the dark-and-light doorway, my hair white now too, Mother. I could hear her move furniture about. Then she dragged a third quilt, the thick, homemade Chinese kind, across me. After that I lost track of her location. I spied from beneath my eyelids and had to hold back a jump. She had pulled up a chair and was sitting by the bed next to my head. I could see her strong hands in her lap, not working fourteen pairs of needles. She is very proud of her hands, which can make anything and stay pink and soft while my father's became like carved wood. Her palm lines do not branch into head, heart, and life lines like other people's but crease with just one atavistic fold. That night she was a sad bear; a great sheep in a wool shawl. She recently took to wearing shawls and granny glasses, American fashions. What did she want, sitting there so large next to my head? I could feel her stare—her eyes two lights warm on my graying hair, then on the creases at the sides of my mouth, my thin neck, my thin cheeks, my thin arms. I felt her sight warm each of my bony elbows, and I flopped about in my fake sleep to hide them from her criticism. She sent light at full brightness beaming through my eyelids, her eyes at my eyes, and I had to open them.

"What's the matter, Mama? Why are you sitting there?"

She reached over and switched on a lamp she had placed on the floor beside her. "I swallowed that LSD pill you left on the kitchen counter," she announced.

"That wasn't LSD, Mama. It was just a cold pill. I have a cold."

"You're always catching colds when you come home. You must be eating too much *yin*. Let me get you another quilt."

"No, no more quilts. You shouldn't take pills that aren't prescribed for you. 'Don't eat pills you find on the curb,' you always told us."

"You children never tell me what you're really up to. How else am I going to find out what you're really up to?" As if her head hurt, she closed her eyes behind the gold wire rims. "Aiaa," she sighed, "how can I bear to have you leave me again?"

How can I bear to leave her again? She would close up this room, open temporarily for me, and wander about cleaning and cleaning the shrunken house, so tidy since our leaving. Each chair has its place now. And the sinks in the bedrooms work, their alcoves no longer stuffed with laundry right up to the ceiling. My mother has put the clothes and shoes into boxes, stored against hard times. The sinks had been built of gray marble for the old Chinese men who boarded here before we came. I used to picture modest little old men washing in the mornings and dressing before they shuffled out of these bedrooms. I would have to leave and go again into the world out there which has no marble ledges for my clothes, no quilts made from our own ducks and turkeys, no ghosts of neat little old men.

The lamp gave off the sort of light that comes from a television, which made the high ceiling disappear and then suddenly drop back into place. I could feel that clamping down and see how my mother had pulled the blinds down so low that the bare rollers were showing. No passer-by would detect a daughter in this house. My mother would sometimes be a large animal, barely real in the dark; then she would become a mother again. I could see the wrinkles around her big eyes, and I could see her cheeks sunken without her top teeth.

"I'll be back again soon," I said. "You know that I come back. I think of you when I'm not here."

"Yes, I know you. I know you now. I've always known you. You're the one with the charming words. You have never come back. 'I'll be back on Turkeyday,' you said. Huh."

I shut my teeth together, vocal cords cut, they hurt so. I would not speak words to give her pain. All her children gnash their teeth.

"The last time I saw you, you were still young," she said. "Now you're old."

"It's only been a year since I visited you."

"That's the year you turned old. Look at you, hair gone gray, and you haven't even fattened up yet. I know how the Chinese talk about us. 'They're so poor,' they say, 'they can't afford to fatten up any of their daughters.' 'Years in

America,' they say, 'and they don't eat.' Oh, the shame of it —a whole family of skinny children. And your father—he's so skinny, he's disappearing."

"Don't worry about him, Mama. Doctors are saying that skinny people live longer. Papa's going to live a long time."

"So! I knew I didn't have too many years left. Do you know how I got all this fat? Eating your leftovers. Aiaa, I'm getting so old. Soon you will have no more mother."

"Mama, you've been saying that all my life."

"This time it's true. I'm almost eighty."

"I thought you were only seventy-six."

"My papers are wrong. I'm eighty."

"But I thought your papers are wrong, and you're seventy-two, seventy-three in Chinese years."

"My papers are wrong, and I'm eighty, eighty-one in Chinese years. Seventy. Eighty. What do numbers matter? I'm dropping dead any day now. The aunt down the street was resting on her porch steps, dinner all cooked, waiting for her husband and son to come home and eat it. She closed her eyes for a moment and died. Isn't that a wonderful way to go?"

"But our family lives to be ninety-nine."

"That's your father's family. My mother and father died very young. My youngest sister was an orphan at ten. Our parents were not even fifty."

"Then you should feel grateful you've lived so many extra years."

"I was so sure you were going to be an orphan too. In fact, I'm amazed you've lived to have white hair. Why don't you dye it?"

"Hair color doesn't measure age, Mother. White is just another pigment, like black and brown."

"You're always listening to Teacher Ghosts, those Scientist Ghosts, Doctor Ghosts."

"I have to make a living."

"I never do call you Oldest Daughter. Have you noticed that? I always tell people, 'This is my Biggest Daughter.'"

"Is it true then that Oldest Daughter and Oldest Son died in China? Didn't you tell me when I was ten that she'd have been twenty; when I was twenty, she'd be thirty?" Is that why you've denied me my title?

"No, you must have been dreaming. You must have been making up stories. You are all the children there are."

(Who was that story about—the one where the parents are throwing money at the children, but the children don't pick it up because they're crying too hard? They're writhing on the floor covered with coins. Their parents are going out the door for America, hurling handfuls of change behind them.)

She leaned forward, eyes brimming with what she was about to say: "I work so hard," she said. She was doing her stare—at what? My feet began rubbing together as if to tear each other's skin off. She started talking again, "The tomato vines prickle my hands; I can feel their little stubble hairs right through my gloves. My feet squish-squish in the rotten tomatoes, squish-squish in the tomato mud the feet ahead of me have sucked. And do you know the best way to stop the itch from the tomato hairs? You break open a fresh tomato and wash yourself with it. You cool your face in tomato juice. Oh, but it's the potatoes that will ruin my hands. I'll get rheumatism washing potatoes, squatting over potatoes."

She had taken off the Ace bandages around her legs for the night. The varicose veins stood out.

"Mama, why don't you stop working? You don't have to work anymore. Do you? Do you really have to work like that? Scabbing in the tomato fields?" Her black hair seems filleted with the band of white at its roots. She dyed her hair so that the farmers would hire her. She would walk to Skid Row and stand in line with the hobos, the winos, the junkies, and the Mexicans until the farm buses came and the farmers picked out the workers they wanted. "You have the house," I said. "For food you have Social Security. And urban renewal must have given you something. It was good in a way when they tore down the laundry. Really, Mama, it was. Otherwise Papa would never have retired. You ought to retire too."

"Do you think your father wanted to stop work? Look at his eyes; the brown is going out of his eyes. He has stopped talking. When I go to work, he eats leftovers. He doesn't cook new food," she said, confessing, me maddened at confessions. "Those Urban Renewal Ghosts gave us moving money. It took us seventeen years to get our customers. How could we start all over on moving money, as if we two old people had another seventeen years in us? Aa"—she flipped something aside with her hand—"White Ghosts can't tell Chinese age."

I closed my eyes and breathed evenly, but she could tell I wasn't asleep.

"This is terrible ghost country, where a human being works her life away," she said. "Even the ghosts work, no time for acrobatics. I have not stopped working since the day the ship landed. I was on my feet the moment the babies were out. In China I never even had to hang up my own clothes. I shouldn't have left, but your father couldn't have supported you without me. I'm the one with the big muscles."

"If you hadn't left, there wouldn't have been a me for you two to support. Mama, I'm really sleepy. Do you mind letting me sleep?" I do not believe in old age. I do not believe in getting tired.

"I didn't need muscles in China. I was small in China." She was. The silk dresses she gave me are tiny. You would not think the same person wore them. This mother can carry a hundred pounds of Texas rice up- and downstairs. She could work at the laundry from 6:30 a.m. until midnight, shifting a baby from an ironing table to a shelf between packages, to the display window, where the ghosts tapped on the glass. "I put you babies in the clean places at the laundry, as far away from the germs that fumed out of the ghosts' clothes as I could. Aa, their socks and handkerchiefs choked me. I cough now because of those seventeen years of breathing dust. Tubercular handkerchiefs. Lepers' socks." I thought she had wanted to show off my baby sister in the display window.

In the midnight unsteadiness we were back at the laundry, and my mother was sitting on an orange crate sorting dirty clothes into mountains—a sheet mountain, a white shirt mountain, a dark shirt mountain, a work-pants mountain, a long underwear mountain, a short underwear mountain, a little hill of socks pinned together in pairs, a little hill of handkerchiefs pinned to tags. Surrounding her were candles she burned in daylight, clean yellow diamonds, footlights that ringed her, mysterious masked mother, nose and mouth veiled with a cowboy handkerchief. Before undoing the bundles, my mother would light a tall new candle, which was a luxury, and the pie pans full of old wax and wicks that sometimes sputtered blue, a noise I thought was the germs getting seared.

"No tickee, no washee, mama-san?" a ghost would say, so embarrassing.

"Noisy Red-Mouth Ghost," she'd write on its package, naming it, marking its clothes with its name.

Back in the bedroom I said, "The candles must have helped. It was a good idea of yours to use candles."

"They didn't do much good. All I have to do is think about dust sifting out of clothes or peat dirt blowing across a field or chick mash falling from a scoop, and I start coughing." She coughed deeply. "See what I mean? I have worked too much. Human beings don't work like this in China. Time goes slower there. Here we have to hurry, feed the hungry children before we're too old to work. I feel like a mother cat hunting for its kittens. She has to find them fast because in a few hours she will forget how to count or that she had any kittens at all. I can't sleep in this country because it doesn't shut down for the night. Factories, canneries, restaurants—always somebody somewhere working through the night. It never gets done all at once here. Time was different in China. One year lasted as long as my total time here; one evening so long, you could visit your women friends, drink tea, and play cards at each house, and it would still be twilight. It even got boring, nothing to do but fan ourselves. Here midnight comes and the floor's not swept, the ironing's not ready, the money's not made. I would still be young if we lived in China."

"Time is the same from place to place," I said unfeelingly. "There is only the eternal present, and biology. The reason you feel time pushing is that you had six children after you were forty-five and you worried about raising us. You shouldn't worry anymore, though, Mama. You should feel good you had so many babies around you in middle age. Not many mothers have that. Wasn't it like prolonging youth? Now wasn't it? You mustn't worry now. All of us have grown up. And you can stop working."

"I can't stop working. When I stop working, I hurt. My head, my back, my legs hurt. I get dizzy. I can't stop."

"I'm like that too, Mama. I work all the time. Don't worry about me starving. I won't starve. I know how to work. I work all the time. I know how to kill food, how to skin and pluck it. I know how to keep warm by sweeping and mopping. I know how to work when things get bad."

"It's a good thing I taught you children to look after yourselves. We're not going back to China for sure now."

"You've been saying that since nineteen forty-nine."

"Now it's final. We got a letter from the villagers yesterday. They asked if it was all right with us that they took over the land. The last uncles have been killed so your father is the only person left to say it is all right, you see. He has written saying they can have it. So. We have no more China to go home to."

It must be all over then. My mother and father have stoked each other's indignation for almost forty years telling stories about land quarrels among the uncles, the inlaws, the grandparents. Episodes from their various points of view came weekly in the mail, until the uncles were executed kneeling on broken glass by people who had still other plans for the land. How simply it ended—my father writing his permission. Permission asked, permission given twenty-five years after the Revolution.

"We belong to the planet now, Mama. Does it make sense to you that if we're no longer attached to one piece of land, we belong to the planet? Wherever we happen to be standing, why, that spot belongs to us as much as any other spot." Can we spend the fare money on furniture and cars? Will American flowers smell good now?

"I don't want to go back anyway," she said. "I've gotten used to eating. And the Communists are much too mischievous. You should see the ones I meet in the fields. They bring sacks under their clothes to steal grapes and tomatoes from the growers. They come with trucks on Sundays. And they're killing each other in San Francisco." One of the old men caught his visitor, another old fellow, stealing his bantam; the owner spotted its black feet sticking out of his guest's sweater. We woke up one morning to find a hole in the ground where our loquat tree had stood. Later we saw a new loquat tree most similar to ours in a Chinese neighbor's yard. We knew a family who had a sign in their vegetable patch: "Since this is not a Communist garden but cabbages grown by private enterprise, please do not steal from my garden." It was dated and signed in good handwriting.

"The new immigrants aren't Communists, Mother. They're fugitives from the real Communists."

"They're Chinese, and Chinese are mischievous. No, I'm too old to keep up with them. They'd be too clever for me. I've lost my cunning, having grown accustomed to food, you see. There's only one thing that I really want anymore. I want you here, not wandering like a ghost from Romany. I want every one of you living here together. When you're all home, all six of you with your children and husbands and wives, there are twenty or thirty people in this house. Then I'm happy. And your father is happy. Whichever room I walk into overflows with my relatives, grand-sons, sons-in-law. I can't turn around without touching somebody. That's the way a house should be." Her eyes are big, inconsolable. A spider headache spreads out in fine branches over my skull. She is etching spider legs into the icy bone. She pries open my head and my fists and crams into them responsibility for time, responsibility for inter-vening oceans.

The gods pay her and my father back for leaving their parents. My grandmother wrote letters pleading for them to come home, and they ignored her. Now they know how she felt.

"When I'm away from here," I had to tell her, "I don't get sick. I don't go to the hospital every holiday. I don't get pneumonia, no dark spots on my x-rays. My chest doesn't hurt when I breathe. I can breathe. And I don't get head-aches at 3:00. I don't have to take medicines or go to doc-tors. Elsewhere I don't have to lock my doors and keep checking the locks. I don't stand at the windows and watch for movements and see them in the dark."

"What do you mean you don't lock your doors?"

"I do. I do. But not the way I do here. I don't hear ghost sounds. I don't stay awake listening to walking in the kitchen. I don't hear the doors and windows unhinging."

"It was probably just a Wino Ghost or a Hobo Ghost looking for a place to sleep."

"I don't want to hear Wino Ghosts and Hobo Ghosts. I've found some places in this country that are ghost-free. And I think I belong there, where I don't catch colds or use my hospitalization insurance. Here I'm sick so often, I can barely work. I can't help it, Mama."

She yawned. "It's better, then, for you to stay away. The weather in California must not agree with you. You can come for visits." She got up and turned off the light. "Of course, you must go, Little Dog."

A weight lifted from me. The quilts must be filling with air. The world is somehow lighter. She has not called me that endearment for years—a name to fool the gods. I am really a Dragon, as she is a Dragon, both of us born in dragon years. I am practically a first daughter of a first daughter.

"Good night, Little Dog."

"Good night, Mother."

She sends me on my way, working always and now old, dreaming the dreams about shrinking babies and the sky covered with airplanes and a Chinatown bigger than the ones here.

At

the

Western

Palace

When she was about sixty-eight years old, Brave Orchid took a day off to wait at San Francisco International Airport for the plane that was bringing her sister to the United States. She had not seen Moon Orchid for thirty years. She had begun this waiting at home, getting up a half-hour before Moon Orchid's plane took off in Hong Kong. Brave Orchid would add her will power to the forces that keep an airplane up. Her head hurt with the concentration. The plane had to be light, so no matter how tired she felt, she dared not rest her spirit on a wing but continuously and gently pushed up on the plane's belly. She had already been waiting at the airport for nine hours. She was wakeful.

Next to Brave Orchid sat Moon Orchid's only daughter, who was helping her aunt wait. Brave Orchid had made two of her own children come too because they could drive, but they had been lured away by the magazine racks and the gift shops and coffee shops. Her American children could not sit for very long. They did not understand sitting; they had wandering feet. She hoped they would get back from the pay t.v.'s or the pay toilets or wherever they were spending their money before the plane arrived. If they did not come back soon, she would go look for them. If her son thought he could hide in the men's room, he was wrong.

"Are you all right, Aunt?" asked her niece.

"No, this chair hurts me. Help me pull some chairs together so I can put my feet up."

She unbundled a blanket and spread it out to make a bed for herself. On the floor she had two shopping bags full of canned peaches, real peaches, beans wrapped in taro leaves, cookies, Thermos bottles, enough food for everybody, though only her niece would eat with her. Her bad boy and bad girl were probably sneaking hamburgers, wasting their money. She would scold them.

Many soldiers and sailors sat about, oddly calm, like little boys in cowboy uniforms. (She thought "cowboy" was what you would call a Boy Scout.) They should have been crying hysterically on their way to Vietnam. "If I see one that looks Chinese," she thought, "I'll go over and give him some advice." She sat up suddenly; she had forgotten about her own son, who was even now in Vietnam. Carefully she split her attention, beaming half of it to the ocean, into the water to keep him afloat. He was on a ship. He was in Vietnamese waters. She was sure of it. He and the other children were lying to her. They had said he was in Japan, and then they said he was in the Philippines. But when she sent him her help, she could feel that he was on a ship in Da Nang. Also she had seen the children hide the envelopes that his letters came in.

"Do you think my son is in Vietnam?" she asked her niece, who was dutifully eating.

"No. Didn't your children say he was in the Philippines?"

"Have you ever seen any of his letters with Philippine stamps on them?"

"Oh, yes. Your children showed me one."

"I wouldn't put it past them to send the letters to some Filipino they know. He puts Manila postmarks on them to fool me."

"Yes, I can imagine them doing that. But don't worry. Your son can take care of himself. All your children can take care of themselves."

"Not him. He's not like other people. Not normal at all. He sticks erasers in his ears, and the erasers are still attached to the pencil stubs. The captain will say, 'Abandon ship,' or, 'Watch out for bombs,' and he won't hear. He doesn't listen to orders. I told him to flee to Canada, but he wouldn't go."

She closed her eyes. After a short while, plane and ship under control, she looked again at the children in uniforms. Some of the blond ones looked like baby chicks, their crew cuts like the downy yellow on baby chicks. You had to feel sorry for them even though they were Army and Navy Ghosts.

Suddenly her son and daughter came running. "Come, Mother. The plane's landed early. She's here already." They hurried, folding up their mother's encampment. She was glad her children were not useless. They must have known what this trip to San Francisco was about then. "It's a good thing I made you come early," she said.

Brave Orchid pushed to the front of the crowd. She had to be in front. The passengers were separated from the people waiting for them by glass doors and walls. Immigration Ghosts were stamping papers. The travellers crowded along some conveyor belts to have their luggage searched. Brave Orchid did not see her sister anywhere. She stood watching for four hours. Her children left and came back. "Why don't you sit down?" they asked.

"The chairs are too far away," she said.

"Why don't you sit on the floor then?"

No, she would stand, as her sister was probably standing in a line she could not see from here. Her American children had no feelings and no memory.

To while away time, she and her niece talked about the Chinese passengers. These new immigrants had it easy. On Ellis Island the people were thin after forty days at sea and had no fancy luggage.

"That one looks like her," Brave Orchid would say.

"No, that's not her."

Ellis Island had been made out of wood and iron. Here everything was new plastic, a ghost trick to lure immigrants into feeling safe and spilling their secrets. Then the Alien Office could send them right back. Otherwise, why did they lock her out, not letting her help her sister answer questions and spell her name? At Ellis Island when the ghost asked Brave Orchid what year her husband had cut off his pigtail, a Chinese who was crouching on the floor motioned her not to talk. "I don't know," she had said. If it weren't for that Chinese man, she might not be here today, or her husband either. She hoped some Chinese, a janitor or a clerk, would look out for Moon Orchid. Luggage conveyors fooled immigrants into thinking the Gold Mountain was going to be easy.

Brave Orchid felt her heart jump—Moon Orchid. "There she is," she shouted. But her niece saw it was not her mother at all. And it shocked her to discover the woman her aunt was pointing out. This was a young woman, younger than herself, no older than Moon Orchid the day the sisters parted. "Moon Orchid will have changed a little, of course," Brave Orchid was saying. "She will have learned to wear western clothes." The woman wore a navy blue suit with a bunch of dark cherries at the shoulder.

"No, Aunt," said the niece. "That's not my mother."

"Perhaps not. It's been so many years. Yes, it is your mother. It must be. Let her come closer, and we can tell. Do you think she's too far away for me to tell, or is it my eyes getting bad?"

"It's too many years gone by," said the niece.

Brave Orchid turned suddenly—another Moon Orchid, this one a neat little woman with a bun. She was laughing at something the person ahead of her in line said. Moon Orchid was just like that, laughing at nothing. "I would be able to tell the difference if one of them would only come closer," Brave Orchid said with tears, which she did not wipe. Two children met the woman with the cherries, and she shook their hands. The other woman was met by a young man. They looked at each other gladly, then walked away side by side.

Up close neither one of those women looked like Moon Orchid at all. "Don't worry, Aunt," said the niece. "I'll know her."

"I'll know her too. I knew her before you did."

The niece said nothing, although she had seen her mother only five years ago. Her aunt liked having the last word.

Finally Brave Orchid's children quit wandering and drooped on a railing. Who knew what they were thinking? At last the niece called out, "I see her! I see her! Mother! Mother!" Whenever the doors parted, she shouted, probably embarrassing the American cousins, but she didn't care. She called out, "Mama! Mama!" until the crack in the sliding doors became too small to let in her voice. "Mama!" What a strange word in an adult voice. Many people turned to see what adult was calling, "Mama!" like a child. Brave Orchid saw an old, old woman jerk her head up, her little eyes blinking confusedly, a woman whose nerves leapt toward the sound anytime she heard "Mama!" Then she relaxed to her own business again. She was a tiny, tiny lady, very thin, with little fluttering hands, and her hair was in a gray knot. She was dressed in a gray wool suit; she wore pearls around her neck and in her earlobes. Moon Orchid *would* travel with her jewels showing. Brave Orchid momentarily saw, like a larger, younger outline around this old woman, the sister she had been waiting for. The familiar dim halo faded, leaving the woman so old, so gray. So old. Brave Orchid pressed against the glass. *That* old lady? Yes, that old lady facing the ghost who stamped her papers without questioning her was her sister. Then, without noticing her family, Moon Orchid walked smiling over to the Suitcase Inspector Ghost, who took her boxes apart, pulling out puffs of tissue. From where she was, Brave Orchid could not see what her sister had chosen to carry across the ocean. She wished her sister would look her way. Brave Orchid thought that if *she* were entering a new country, she would be at the windows. Instead Moon Orchid hovered over the unwrapping, surprised at each reappearance as if she were opening presents after a birthday party.

"Mama!" Moon Orchid's daughter kept calling. Brave Orchid said to her children, "Why don't you call your aunt too? Maybe she'll hear us if all of you call out together." But her children slunk away. Maybe that shame-face they so often wore was American politeness.

"Mama!" Moon Orchid's daughter called again, and this time her mother looked right at her. She left her bundles in a heap and came running. "Hey!" the Customs Ghost yelled at her. She went back to clear up her mess, talking inaudibly to her daughter all the while. Her daughter pointed toward Brave Orchid. And at last Moon Orchid looked at her—two old women with faces like mirrors.

Their hands reached out as if to touch the other's face, then returned to their own, the fingers checking the grooves in the forehead and along the sides of the mouth. Moon Orchid, who never understood the gravity of things, started smiling and laughing, pointing at Brave Orchid. Finally Moon Orchid gathered up her stuff, strings hanging and papers loose, and met her sister at the door, where they shook hands, oblivious to blocking the way.

"You're an old woman," said Brave Orchid.

"Aiaa. *You're* an old woman."

"But you are really old. Surely, you can't say that about me. I'm not old the way you're old."

"But *you* really are old. You're one year older than I am."

"Your hair is white and your face all wrinkled."

"You're so skinny."

"You're so fat."

"Fat women are more beautiful than skinny women."

The children pulled them out of the doorway. One of Brave Orchid's children brought the car from the parking lot, and the other heaved the luggage into the trunk. They put the two old ladies and the niece in the back seat. All the way home—across the Bay Bridge, over the Diablo hills, across the San Joaquin River to the valley, the valley moon so white at dusk—all the way home, the two sisters exclaimed every time they turned to look at each other, "Aiaa! How old!"

Brave Orchid forgot that she got sick in cars, that all vehicles but palanquins made her dizzy. "You're so old," she kept saying. "How did you get so old?"

Brave Orchid had tears in her eyes. But Moon Orchid said, "You look older than I. You *are* older than I," and again she'd laugh. "You're wearing an old mask to tease me." It surprised Brave Orchid that after thirty years she could still get annoyed at her sister's silliness.

Brave Orchid's husband was waiting under the tangerine tree. Moon Orchid recognized him as the brother-in-law in photographs, not as the young man who left on a ship. Her sister had married the ideal in masculine beauty, the thin scholar with the hollow cheeks and the long fingers. And here he was, an old man, opening the gate he had built with his own hands, his hair blowing silver in twilight. "Hello," he said like an Englishman in Hong Kong. "Hello," she said like an English telephone operator. He went to help his children unload the car, gripping the suitcase handles in his bony fingers, his bony wrists locked.

Brave Orchid's husband and children brought everything into the dining room, provisions for a lifetime move heaped all over the floor and furniture. Brave Orchid wanted to have a luck ceremony and then to put things away where they belonged, but Moon Orchid said, "I've got presents for everybody. Let me get them." She opened her boxes again. Her suitcase lids gaped like mouths; Brave Orchid had better hurry with the luck.

"First I've got shoes for all of you from Lovely Orchid," Moon Orchid said, handing them out to her nieces and nephews, who grimaced at one another. Lovely Orchid, the youngest aunt, owned either a shoe store or a shoe factory in Hong Kong. That was why every Christmas she sent a dozen pairs, glittering with yellow and pink plastic beads, sequins, and turquoise blue flowers. "She must give us the leftovers," Brave Orchid's children were saying in English.

As Brave Orchid ran back and forth turning on all the lights, every lamp and bulb, she glared sideways at her children. They would be sorry when they had to walk barefoot through snow and rocks because they didn't take what shoes they could, even if the wrong size. She would put the slippers next to the bathtub on the linoleum floors in winter and trick her lazy children into wearing them.

"May I have some scissors? Oh, where are my scissors?" said Moon Orchid. She slit the heel of a black embroidered slipper and pulled out the cotton—which was entangled with jewels. "You'll have to let me pierce your ears," she told her nieces, rubbing their earlobes. "Then you can wear these." There were earrings with skewers like gold krisses. There was a jade heart and an opal. Brave Orchid interrupted her dashing about to rub the stones against her skin.

Moon Orchid laughed softly in delight. "And look here. Look here," she said. She was holding up a paper warrior-saint, and he was all intricacies and light. A Communist had cut a wisp of black paper into a hero with sleeves like butterflies' wings and with tassels and flags, which fluttered when you breathed on him. "Did someone really cut this out by hand?" the children kept asking. "Really?" The eyebrows and mustache, the fierce wrinkles between the eyes, the face, all were the merest black webs. His open hand had been cut out finger by finger. Through the spaces you could see light and the room and each other. "Oh, there's more. There's more," said Moon Orchid happily. She picked up another paper cutout and blew on it. It was the scholar who always carries a fan; her breath shook its blue feathers. His brush and quill and scrolls tied with ribbon jutted out of lace vases. "And more"—an orange warrior-poet with sword and scroll; a purple knight with doily armor, holes for scales; a wonderful archer on a red horse with a mane like fire; a modern Communist worker with a proud gold hammer; a girl Communist soldier with pink pigtails and pink rifle. "And this is Fa Mu Lan," she said. "She was a woman warrior, and really existed." Fa Mu Lan was green and beautiful, and her robes whirled out as she drew her sword.

"Paper dolls," said Brave Orchid to her children. "I'd have thought you were too old to be playing with dolls." How greedy to play with presents in front of the giver. How impolite ("untraditional" in Chinese) her children were. With a slam of her cleaver, she cracked rock candy into jagged pieces. "Take some," she urged. "Take more." She brought the yellow crystals on a red paper plate to her family, one by one. It was very important that the beginning be sweet. Her children acted as if this eating were a bother. "Oh, all right," they said, and took the smallest slivers. Who would think that children could dislike candy? It was abnormal, not in the nature of children, not human. "Take a big piece," she scolded. She'd make them eat it like medicine if necessary. They were so stupid, surely they weren't adults yet. They'd put the bad mouth on their aunt's first American day; you had to sweeten their noisy barbarous mouths. She opened the front door and mumbled something. She opened the back door and mumbled something.

"What do you say when you open the door like that?" her children used to ask when they were younger.

"Nothing. Nothing," she would answer.

"Is it spirits, Mother? Do you talk to spirits? Are you asking them in or asking them out?"

"It's nothing," she said. She never explained anything that was really important. They no longer asked.

When she came back from talking to the invisibilities, Brave Orchid saw that her sister was strewing the room. The paper people clung flat against the lampshades, the chairs, the tablecloths. Moon Orchid left fans unfolded and dragons with accordion bodies dangling from doorknobs. She was unrolling white silk. "Men are good at stitching roosters," she was pointing out bird embroidery. It was amazing how a person could grow old without learning to put things away.

"Let's put these things away," Brave Orchid said.

"Oh, Sister," said Moon Orchid. "Look what I have for you," and she held up a pale green silk dress lined in wool. "In winter you can look like summer and be warm like summer." She unbuttoned the frogs to show the lining, thick and plaid like a blanket.

"Now where would I wear such a fancy dress?" said Brave Orchid. "Give it to one of the children."

"I have bracelets and earrings for them."

"They're too young for jewelry. They'll lose it."

"They seem very big for children."

"The girls broke six jade bracelets playing baseball. And they can't endure pain. They scream when I squeeze their hands into the jade. Then that very day, they'll break it. We'll put the jewelry in the bank, and we'll buy glass and black wood frames for the silk scrolls." She bundled up the sticks that opened into flowers. "What were you doing carrying these scraps across the ocean?"

Brave Orchid took what was useful and solid into the back bedroom, where Moon Orchid would stay until they decided what she would do permanently. Moon Orchid picked up pieces of string, but bright colors and movements distracted her. "Oh, look at this," she'd say. "Just look at this. You have carp." She was turning the light off and on in the goldfish tank, which sat in the rolltop desk that Brave Orchid's husband had taken from the gambling house when it shut down during World War II. Moon Orchid looked up at the grandparents' photographs that hung on the wall above the desk. Then she turned around and looked at the opposite wall; there, equally large, were pictures of Brave Orchid and her husband. They had put up their own pictures because later the children would not have the sense to do it.

"Oh, look," said Moon Orchid. "Your pictures are up too. Why is that?"

"No reason. Nothing," said Brave Orchid. "In America you can put up anybody's picture you like."

On the shelf of the rolltop desk, like a mantel under

the grandparents' photos, there were bowls of plastic tangerines and oranges, crepe-paper flowers, plastic vases, porcelain vases filled with sand and incense sticks. A clock sat on a white runner crocheted with red phoenixes and red words about how lucky and bright life is. Moon Orchid lifted the ruffles to look inside the pigeon holes. There were also pen trays and little drawers, enough so that the children could each have one or two for their very own. The fish tank took up half the desk space, and there was still room for writing. The rolltop was gone; the children had broken it slat by slat when they hid inside the desk, pulling the top over themselves. The knee hole had boxes of toys that the married children's children played with now. Brave Orchid's husband had padlocked one large bottom cabinet and one drawer.

"Why do you keep it locked?" Moon Orchid asked. "What's in here?"

"Nothing," he said. "Nothing."

"If you want to poke around," said Brave Orchid, "why don't you find out what's in the kitchen drawers so you can help me cook?"

They cooked enough food to cover the dining room and kitchen tables. "Eat!" Brave Orchid ordered. "Eat!" She would not allow anybody to talk while eating. In some families the children worked out a sign language, but here the children spoke English, which their parents didn't seem to hear.

After they ate and cleaned up, Brave Orchid said, "Now! We have to get down to business."

"What do you mean?" said her sister. She and her daughter held one another's hands.

"Oh, no. I don't want to listen to this," said Brave Orchid's husband, and left to read in bed.

The three women sat in the enormous kitchen with the butcher's block and two refrigerators. Brave Orchid had an inside stove in the kitchen and a stove outside on the back porch. All day long the outside stove cooked peelings and gristle into chicken feed. It horrified the children when they caught her throwing scraps of chicken into the chicken feed. Both stoves had been turned off for the night now, and the air was cooling.

"Wait until morning, Aunt," said Moon Orchid's daughter. "Let her get some sleep."

"Yes, I do need rest after travelling all the way from China," she said. "I'm here. You've done it and brought me here." Moon Orchid meant that they should be satisfied with what they had already accomplished. Indeed, she stretched happily and appeared quite satisfied to be sitting in that kitchen at that moment. "I want to go to sleep early because of jet lag," she said, but Brave Orchid, who had never been on an airplane, did not let her.

"What are we going to do about your husband?" Brave Orchid asked quickly. That ought to wake her up.

"I don't know. Do we have to do something?"

"He does not know you're here."

Moon Orchid did not say anything. For thirty years she had been receiving money from him from America. But she had never told him that she wanted to come to the United States. She waited for him to suggest it, but he never did. Nor did she tell him that her sister had been working for years to transport her here. First Brave Orchid had found a Chinese-American husband for her daughter. Then the daughter had come and had been able to sign the papers to bring Moon Orchid over.

"We have to tell him you've arrived," said Brave Orchid.

Moon Orchid's eyes got big like a child's. "I shouldn't be here," she said.

"Nonsense. I want you here, and your daughter wants you here."

"But that's all."

"Your husband is going to have to see you. We'll make him recognize you. Ha. Won't it be fun to see his face? You'll go to his house. And when his second wife answers the door, you say, 'I want to speak to my husband,' and you name his personal name. 'Tell him I'll be sitting in the family room.' Walk past her as if she were a servant. She'll scold him when he comes home from work, and it'll serve him right. You yell at him too."

"I'm scared," said Moon Orchid. "I want to go back to Hong Kong."

"You can't. It's too late. You've sold your apartment. See here. We know his address. He's living in Los Angeles with his second wife, and they have three children. Claim your rights. Those are *your* children. He's got two sons. *You* have two sons. You take them away from her. You become their mother."

"Do you really think I can be a mother of sons? Don't you think they'll be loyal to her, since she gave birth to them?"

"The children will go to their true mother—you," said Brave Orchid. "That's the way it is with mothers and children."

"Do you think he'll get angry at me because I came without telling him?"

"He deserves your getting angry with him. For abandoning you and for abandoning your daughter."

"He didn't abandon me. He's given me so much money. I've had all the food and clothes and servants I've ever wanted. And he's supported our daughter too, even though she's only a girl. He sent her to college. I can't bother him. I mustn't bother him."

"How can you let him get away with this? Bother him. He deserves to be bothered. How dare he marry somebody else when he has you? How can you sit there so calmly? He would've let you stay in China forever. *I* had to send for your daughter, and *I* had to send for you. Urge her," she turned to her niece. "Urge her to go look for him."

"I think you should go look for my father," she said. "I'd like to meet him. I'd like to see what my father looks like."

"What does it matter what he's like?" said her mother. "You're a grown woman with a husband and children of your own. You don't need a father—or a mother either. You're only curious."

"In this country," said Brave Orchid, "many people make their daughters their heirs. If you don't go see him, he'll give everything to the second wife's children."

"But he gives us everything anyway. What more do I have to ask for? If I see him face to face, what is there to say?"

"I can think of hundreds of things," said Brave Orchid. "Oh, how I'd love to be in your place. I could tell him so many things. What scenes I could make. You're so wishy-washy."

"Yes, I am."

"You have to ask him why he didn't come home. Why he turned into a barbarian. Make him feel bad about leaving his mother and father. Scare him. Walk right into his house with your suitcases and boxes. Move right into the bedroom. Throw her stuff out of the drawers and put yours in. Say, 'I am the first wife, and she is our servant.'"

"Oh, no, I can't do that. I can't do that at all. That's terrible."

"Of course you can. I'll teach you. 'I am the first wife, and she is our servant.' And you teach the little boys to call you Mother."

"I don't think I'd be very good with little boys. Little American boys. Our brother is the only boy I've known. Aren't they very rough and unfeeling?"

"Yes, but they're yours. Another thing I'd do if I were you, I'd get a job and help him out. Show him I could make his life easier; how I didn't need his money."

"He has a great deal of money, doesn't he?"

"Yes, he can do some job the barbarians value greatly."

"Could I find a job like that? I've never had a job."

"You could be a maid in a hotel," Brave Orchid advised. "A lot of immigrants start that way nowadays. And the maids get to bring home all the leftover soap and the clothes people leave behind."

"I would clean up after people, then?"

Brave Orchid looked at this delicate sister. She was such a little old lady. She had long fingers and thin, soft hands. And she had a high-class city accent from living in Hong Kong. Not a trace of village accent remained; she had been away from the village for that long. But Brave Orchid would not relent; her dainty sister would just have to toughen up. "Immigrants also work in the canneries, where it's so noisy it doesn't matter if they speak Chinese or what. The easiest way to find a job, though, is to work in Chinatown. You get twenty-five cents an hour and all your meals if you're working in a restaurant."

If she were in her sister's place, Brave Orchid would have been on the phone immediately, demanding one of those Chinatown jobs. She would make the boss agree that she start work as soon as he opened his doors the next morning. Immigrants nowadays were bandits, beating up store owners and stealing from them rather than working. It must've been the Communuists who taught them those habits.

Moon Orchid rubbed her forehead. The kitchen light shined warmly on the gold and jade rings that gave her hands a completeness. One of the rings was a wedding ring. Brave Orchid, who had been married for almost fifty years, did not wear any rings. They got in the way of all the work. She did not want the gold to wash away in the dishwater and the laundry water and the field water. She looked at her younger sister whose very wrinkles were fine. "Forget about a job," she said, which was very lenient of her. "You won't have to work. You just go to your husband's house and demand your rights as First Wife. When you see him, you can say, 'Do you remember me?' "

"What if he doesn't?"

"Then start telling him details about your life together in China. Act like a fortuneteller. He'll be so impressed."

"Do you think he'll be glad to see me?"

"He better be glad to see you."

As midnight came, twenty-two hours after she left Hong Kong, Moon Orchid began to tell her sister that she really was going to face her husband. "He won't like me," she said.

"Maybe you should dye your hair black, so he won't think you're old. Or I have a wig you can borrow. On the other hand, he should see how you've suffered. Yes, let him see how he's made your hair turn white."

These many hours, her daughter held Moon Orchid's hand. The two of them had been separated for five years. Brave Orchid had mailed the daughter's young photograph to a rich and angry man with citizenship papers. He was a tyrant. Mother and daughter were sorry for one another. "Let's not talk about this anymore," said Moon Orchid. "We can plan tomorrow. I want to hear about my grandchildren. Tell me about them. I have three grandchildren, don't I?" she asked her daughter.

Brave Orchid thought that her niece was like her mother, the lovely, useless type. She had spent so much time trying to toughen up these two. "The children are very smart, Mother," her niece was saying. "The teachers say they are brilliant. They can speak Chinese and English. They'll be able to talk to you."

"My children can talk to you too," said Brave Orchid. "Come. Talk to your aunt," she ordered.

Her sons and daughters mumbled and disappeared—into the bathroom, the basement, the various hiding places they had dug throughout the house. One of them locked herself in the pantry-storeroom, where she had cleared off a shelf for a desk among the food. Brave Orchid's children were antisocial and secretive. Ever since they were babies, they had burrowed little nests for themselves in closets and underneath stairs; they made tents under tables and behind doors. "My children are also very bright," she said. "Let me show you before you go to sleep." She took her sister to the living room where she had a glass case, a large upside-down fish tank, and inside were her children's athletic trophies and scholarship trophies. There was even a beauty contest trophy. She had decorated them with runners about luck.

"Oh my, isn't that wonderful?" said the aunt. "You must be so proud of them. Your children must be so smart." The children who were in the living room groaned and left. Brave Orchid did not understand why they were ashamed of the things they could do. It was hard to believe that they could do the things the trophies said they did. Maybe they had stolen them from the real winners. Maybe they had bought cups and medallions and pretended they'd won them. She'd have to accuse them and see how they reacted. Perhaps they fooled the Ghost Teachers and Ghost Coaches, who couldn't tell smart Chinese from dumb Chinese. Her children certainly didn't seem like much.

She made some of the children sleep on the floor and put Moon Orchid and her daughter in their room. "Will my mother be living at your house or my house?" her niece asked Brave Orchid.

"She's going to live with her own husband." Brave Orchid was firm. She would not forget about this subject in the morning.

The next day, immediately after breakfast, Brave Orchid talked about driving to Los Angeles. They would not take the coast route along mountainsides that dropped into the sea—the way her children, who liked carnival rides, would want to go. She would make them take the inland route, flat and direct.

"The first thing you've got to ask your husband," she said, "is why he never came back to China when he got rich."

"All right," said Moon Orchid. She was poking about the house, holding cans up to her ear, trailing after the children.

"He probably has a car," Brave Orchid persisted. "He can drive you places. Should he tell you to go away, turn around at the door and say, 'May I come and watch your television now and then?' Oh, wouldn't that be pathetic? But he won't kick you out. No, he won't. You walk right into the bedroom, and you open the second wife's closet. Take whatever clothes you like. That will give you an American wardrobe."

"Oh, I can't do that."

"You can! You can! Take First Sister-in-Law as your example." Their only brother had had a first wife in the village, but he took a second wife in Singapore, where he had gone to make his gold. Big Wife suffered during the Revolution. "The Communists will kill me," she wrote to her husband, "and you're having fun in Singapore." Little Wife felt so sorry for her, she reminded her husband that he owed it to Big Wife to get her out of China before it was too late. Little Wife saved the passage fare and did the paper work. But when Big Wife came, she chased Little Wife out of the house. There was nothing for their husband to do but build a second house, one for each wife and the children of each wife. They did get together, however, for yearly family portraits. Their sons' first and second wives were also in the pictures, first wives next to the husbands and second wives standing among the children. "Copy our sister-in-law," Brave Orchid instructed. "Make life unbearable for the second wife, and she'll leave. He'll have to build her a second house."

"I wouldn't mind if she stays," said Moon Orchid. "She can comb my hair and keep house. She can wash the dishes and serve our meals. And she can take care of the little boys." Moon Orchid laughed. Again it occurred to Brave Orchid that her sister wasn't very bright, and she had not gotten any smarter in the last thirty years.

"You must make it plain to your husband right at the start what you expect of him. That is what a wife is for —to scold her husband into becoming a good man. Tell him there will be no third wife. Tell him you may go visiting anytime you please. And I, the big sister, may visit your house for as long as I please. Let him know exactly how much money you expect for allowance."

"Should I ask for more or less money now that I'm here?"

"More, of course. Food costs more here. Tell him that your daughter, who is the oldest, must inherit his property. You have to establish these things at the start. Don't begin meek."

Sometimes Moon Orchid seemed to listen too readily—as if her sister were only talking-story. "Have you seen him in all these years?" she asked Brave Orchid.

"No. The last time I saw him was in China—with you. What a terrible, ugly man he must be not to send for you. I'll bet he's hoping you'd be satisfied with his money. How evil he is. You've had to live like a widow for thirty years. You're lucky he didn't have his second wife write you telling you he's dead."

"Oh, no, he wouldn't do that."

"Of course not. He would be afraid of cursing himself."

"But if he is so ugly and mean, maybe I shouldn't bother with him."

"I remember him," said her daughter. "He wrote me a nice letter."

"You can't remember him," said her mother. "You were an infant when he left. He never writes letters; he only sends money orders."

Moon Orchid hoped that the summer would wear away while her sister talked, that Brave Orchid would then find autumn too cold for travel. Brave Orchid did not enjoy travelling. She found it so nauseating that she was still recovering from the trip to San Francisco. Many of the children were home for the summer, and Moon Orchid tried to figure out which one was which. Brave Orchid had written about them in her letters, and Moon Orchid tried to match them up with the descriptions. There was indeed an oldest girl who was absent-minded and messy. She had an American name that sounded like "Ink" in Chinese. "Ink!" Moon Orchid called out; sure enough, a girl smeared with ink said, "Yes?" Then Brave Orchid worried over a daughter who had the mark of an unlucky woman; yes, there was certainly a girl with an upper lip as curled as Brigitte Bardot's. Moon Orchid rubbed this niece's hands and cold feet. There was a boy Brave Orchid said was thick headed. She had written that when he crawled as a baby his head was so heavy he kept dropping it on the floor. Moon Orchid did indeed see a boy whose head was big, his curls enlarging it, his eyebrows thick and slanted like an opera warrior's. Moon Orchid could not tell whether he was any less quick than the others. None of them were articulate or friendly. Brave Orchid had written about a boy whose oddity it was to stick pencil stubs in his ears. Moon Orchid sneaked up on the boys and lifted their hair to look for pencil stubs. "He hangs upside down from the furniture like a bat," his mother wrote. "And he doesn't obey." Moon Orchid didn't find a boy who looked like a bat, and no stubs, so decided that that boy must be the one in Vietnam. And the nephew with the round face and round eyes was the "inaccessible cliff." She immediately recognized the youngest girl, "the raging billows." "Stop following me around!" she shouted at her aunt. "Quit hanging over my neck!"

"What are you doing?" Moon Orchid would ask. "What are you reading?"

"Nothing!" this girl would yell. "You're breathing on me. Don't breathe on me."

It took Moon Orchid several weeks to figure out just how many children there were because some only visited and did not live at home. Some seemed to be married and had children of their own. The babies that spoke no Chinese at all, she decided, were the grandchildren.

None of Brave Orchid's children was happy like the two real Chinese babies who died. Maybe what was wrong was that they had no Oldest Son and no Oldest Daughter to guide them. "I don't see how any of them could support themselves," Brave Orchid said. "I don't see how anybody could want to marry them." Yet, Moon Orchid noticed, some of them seemed to have a husband or a wife who found them bearable.

"They'll never learn how to work," Brave Orchid complained.

"Maybe they're still playing," said Moon Orchid, although they didn't act playful.

"Say good morning to your aunt," Brave Orchid would order, although some of them were adults. "Say good morning to your aunt," she commanded every morning.

"Good morning, Aunt," they said, turning to face her, staring directly into her face. Even the girls stared at her —like cat-headed birds. Moon Orchid jumped and squirmed when they did that. They looked directly into her eyes as if they were looking for lies. Rude. Accusing. They never lowered their gaze; they hardly blinked.

"Why didn't you teach your girls to be demure?" she ventured.

"Demure!" Brave Orchid yelled. "They *are* demure. They're so demure, they barely talk."

It was true that the children made no conversation. Moon Orchid would try to draw them out. They must have many interesting savage things to say, raised as they'd been in the wilderness. They made rough movements, and their accents were not American exactly, but peasant like their mother's, as if they had come from a village deep inside China. She never saw the girls wear the gowns she had given them. The young, raging one, growled in her sleep, "Leave me alone." Sometimes when the girls were reading or watching television, she crept up behind them with a comb and tried to smooth their hair, but they shook their heads, and they turned and fixed her with those eyes. She wondered what they thought and what they saw when they looked at her like that. She liked coming upon them from the back to avoid being looked at. They were like animals the way they stared.

She hovered over a child who was reading, and she pointed at certain words. "What's that?" she tapped at a section that somebody had underlined or annotated. If the child was being patient, he said, "That's an important part."

"Why is it important?"

"Because it tells the main idea here."

"What's the main idea?"

"I don't know the Chinese words for it."

"They're so clever," Moon Orchid would exclaim. "They're so smart. Isn't it wonderful they know things that can't be said in Chinese?"

"Thank you," the child said. When she complimented them, they agreed with her! Not once did she hear a child deny a compliment.

"You're pretty," she said.

"Thank you, Aunt," they answered. How vain. She marveled at their vanity.

"You play the radio beautifully," she teased, and sure enough, they gave one another puzzled looks. She tried all kinds of compliments, and they never said, "Oh, no, you're too kind. I can't play it at all. I'm stupid. I'm ugly." They were capable children; they could do servants' work. But they were not modest.

"What time is it?" she asked, testing what kinds of minds they had, raised away from civilization. She discovered they could tell time very well. And they knew the Chinese words for "thermometer" and "library."

She saw them eat undercooked meat, and they smelled like cow's milk. At first she thought they were so clumsy, they spilled it on their clothes. But soon she decided they themselves smelled of milk. They were big and smelled of milk; they were young and had white hair.

When Brave Orchid screamed at them to dress better, Moon Orchid defended them, sweet wild animals that they were. "But they enjoy looking like furry animals. That's it, isn't it? You enjoy looking like wild animals, don't you?"

"I don't look like a wild animal!" the child would yell like its mother.

"Like an Indian, then. Right?"

"No!"

Moon Orchid stroked their poor white hair. She tugged

at their sleeves and poked their shoulders and stomachs. It was as if she were seeing how much it took to provoke a savage.

"Stop poking me!" they would roar, except for the girl with the cold hands and feet.

"Mm," she mused. "Now the child is saying, 'Stop poking me.'"

Brave Orchid put her sister to work cleaning and sewing and cooking. Moon Orchid was eager to work, roughing it in the wilderness. But Brave Orchid scolded her, "Can't you go any faster than that?" It infuriated Brave Orchid that her sister held up each dish between thumb and forefinger, squirted detergent on the back and front, and ran water without plugging up the drain. Moon Orchid only laughed when Brave Orchid scolded, "Oh, stop that with the dishes. Here. Take this dress and hem it." But Moon Orchid immediately got the thread tangled and laughed about that.

In the mornings Brave Orchid and her husband arose at 6 a.m. He drank a cup of coffee and walked downtown to open up the laundry. Brave Orchid made breakfast for the children who would take the first laundry shift; the ones going to summer school would take the afternoon and night shifts. She put her husband's breakfast into the food container that she had bought in Chinatown, one dish in each tier of the stack. Some mornings Brave Orchid brought the food to the laundry, and other days she sent it with one of the children, but the children let the soup slosh out when they rode over bumps on their bikes. They dangled the tiers from one handlebar and the rice kettle from the other. They were too lazy to walk. Now that her sister and niece were visiting, Brave Orchid went to the laundry later. "Be sure you heat everything up before serving it to your father," she yelled after her son. "And make him coffee after breakfast. And wash the dishes." He would eat with his father and start work.

She walked her sister and niece to the laundry by way of Chinatown. Brave Orchid pointed out the red, green, and gold Chinese school. From the street they could hear children's voices singing the lesson "I Am a Person of the Middle Nation." In front of one of the benevolent associations, a literate man was chanting the *Gold Mountain News*, which was taped to the window. The listening crowd looked at the pictures and said, "Aiaa."

"So this is the United States," Moon Orchid said. "It certainly looks different from China. I'm glad to see the Americans talk like us."

Brave Orchid was again startled at her sister's denseness. "These aren't the Americans. These are the overseas Chinese."

By the time they got to the laundry, the boiler was screaming hot and the machines were ready. "Don't touch or lean against any machine," Brave Orchid warned her sister. "Your skin would fry and peel off." In the midst of the presses stood the sleeve machine, looking like twin silver spaceships. Brave Orchid's husband fitted the shirt sleeves over it with a karate chop between the shoulder blades. "You mustn't back into that," said Brave Orchid.

"You should start off with an easy job," she said. But all the jobs seemed hard for Moon Orchid, who was wearing stockings and dress shoes and a suit. The buttons on the presses seemed too complicated for her to push—and what if she caught her hands or her head inside a press? She was already playing with the water jets dancing on springs from the ceiling. She could fold towels, Brave Orchid decided, and handkerchiefs, but there would be no clean dry clothes until afternoon. Already the temperature was going up.

"Can you iron?" Brave Orchid asked. Perhaps her sister could do the hand-finishing on the shirts when they came off the machines. This was usually Brave Orchid's husband's job. He had such graceful fingers, so good for folding shirts to fit the cardboard patterns that he had cut from campaign posters and fight and wrestling posters. He finished the shirts with a blue band around each.

"Oh, I'd love to try that," Moon Orchid said. Brave

Orchid gave her sister her husband's shirts to practice on. She showed her how family clothes were marked with the ideograph "middle," which is a box with a line through its center. Moon Orchid tugged at the first shirt for half an hour, and she folded it crooked, the buttonholes not lined up with the buttons at all. When a customer came in, her ironing table next to the little stand with the tickets, she did not say "hello" but giggled, leaving the iron on the shirt until it turned yellow and had to be whitened with peroxide. Then she said it was so hot she couldn't breathe.

"Go take a walk," Brave Orchid said, exasperated. Even the children could work. Both girls and boys could sew. "Free Mending and Buttons," said the lettering on the window. The children could work all of the machines, even when they were little and had to stand on apple crates to reach them.

"Oh, I can't go out into Gold Mountain myself," Moon Orchid said.

"Walk back toward Chinatown," suggested Brave Orchid.

"Oh, come with me, please," Moon Orchid said.

"I have to work," said her sister. Brave Orchid placed an apple crate on the sidewalk in front of the laundry. "You sit out here in the cool air until I have a little time." She hooked the steel pole to the screw that unrolled the awning. "Just keep turning until the shadow covers the crate." It took Moon Orchid another half-hour to do this. She rested after every turn and left the pole hanging.

At noon, when the temperature inside reached one hundred and eleven degrees, Brave Orchid went out to the sidewalk and said, "Let's eat." She had heated the leftovers from breakfast on the little stove at the back of the laundry. In back there was also a bedroom for the nights when they finished packaging too tired to walk home. Then five or six people would crowd into the bed together. Some slept on the ironing tables, and the small children slept on the shelves. The shades would be pulled over the display windows and the door. The laundry would become a cozy new home, almost safe from the night footsteps, the traffic, the city outside. The boiler would rest, and no ghost would know there were Chinese asleep in their laundry. When the children were sick and had to stay home from school, they slept in that bedroom so that Brave Orchid could doctor them. The children said that the boiler, jumping up and down, bursting steam, flames shooting out the bottom, matched their dreams when they had a fever.

After lunch, Brave Orchid asked her husband if he and the children could handle the laundry by themselves. She wanted to take Moon Orchid out for some fun. He said that the load was unusually light today.

The sisters walked back to Chinatown. "We're going to get some more to eat," said Brave Orchid. Moon Orchid accompanied her to a gray building with a large storefront room, overhead fans turning coolly and cement floor cool underfoot. Women at round tables were eating black sea-weed gelatin and talking. They poured Karo syrup on top of the black quivering mass. Brave Orchid seated Moon Orchid and dramatically introduced her, "This is my sister who has come to Gold Mountain to reclaim her husband." Many of the women were fellow villagers; others might as well have been villagers, together so long in California.

"Marvelous. You could blackmail him," the women advised. "Have him arrested if he doesn't take you back."

"Disguise yourself as a mysterious lady and find out how bad he is."

"You've got to do some husband beating, that's what you've got to do."

They were joking about her. Moon Orchid smiled and tried to think of a joke too. The large proprietress in a butcher's apron came out of the kitchen lugging tubs full of more black gelatin. Standing over the tables and smoking a cigarette, she watched her customers eat. It was so cool here, black and light-yellow and brown, and the gelatin was so cool. The door was open to the street, no passers-by but

Chinese, though at the windows the venetian blinds slitted the sunlight as if everyone were hiding. Between helpings the women sat back, waving fans made out of silk, paper, sandalwood, and pandanus fronds. They were like rich women in China with nothing to do.

"Game time," said the proprietress, clearing the tables. The women had only been taking a break from their gambling. They spread ringed hands and mixed the ivory tiles click-clack for the next hemp-bird game. "It's time to go," said Brave Orchid, leading her sister outside. "When you come to America, it's a chance to forget some of the bad Chinese habits. A person could get up one day from the gambling table and find her life over." The gambling women were already caught up in their game, calling out good-byes to the sisters.

They walked past the vegetable, fish, and meat markets —not as abundant as in Canton, the carp not as red, the turtles not as old—and entered the cigar and seed shop. Brave Orchid filled her sister's thin hands with carrot candy, melon candy, and sheets of beef jerky. Business was carried out at one end of the shop, which was long and had benches against two walls. Rows of men sat smoking. Some of them stopped gurgling on their silver or bamboo water pipes to greet the sisters. Moon Orchid remembered many of them from the village; the cigar store owner, who looked like a camel, welcomed her. When Brave Orchid's children were young, they thought he was the Old Man of the North, Santa Claus.

As they walked back to the laundry, Brave Orchid showed her sister where to buy the various groceries and how to avoid Skid Row. "On days when you are not feeling safe, walk around it. But you can walk through it unharmed on your strong days." On weak days you notice bodies on the sidewalk, and you are visible to Panhandler Ghosts and Mugger Ghosts.

Brave Orchid and her husband and children worked hardest in the afternoon when the heat was the worst, all the machines hissing and thumping. Brave Orchid did teach her sister to fold the towels. She placed her at the table where the fan blew most. But finally she sent one of the children to walk her home.

From then on Moon Orchid only visited the laundry late in the day when the towels came out of the dryers. Brave Orchid's husband had to cut a pattern from cardboard so Moon Orchid could fold handkerchiefs uniformly. He gave her a shirt cardboard to measure the towels. She never could work any faster than she did on the first day.

The summer days passed while they talked about going to find Moon Orchid's husband. She felt she accomplished a great deal by folding towels. She spent the evening observing the children. She liked to figure them out. She described them aloud. "Now they're studying again. They read so much. Is it because they have enormous quantities to learn, and they're trying not to be savages? He is picking up his pencil and tapping it on the desk. Then he opens his book to page 168. His eyes begin to read. His eyes go back and forth. They go from left to right, from left to right." This makes her laugh. "How wondrous—eyes reading back and forth. Now he's writing his thoughts down. What's *that* thought?" she asked, pointing.

She followed her nieces and nephews about. She bent over them. "Now she is taking a machine off the shelf. She attaches two metal spiders to it. She plugs in the cord. She cracks an egg against the rim and pours the yolk and white out of the shell into the bowl. She presses a button, and the spiders spin the eggs. What are you making?"

"Aunt, please take your finger out of the batter."

"She says, 'Aunt, please take your finger out of the batter,'" Moon Orchid repeated as she turned to follow another niece walking through the kitchen. "Now what's this one doing? Why, she's sewing a dress. She's going to try it on." Moon Orchid would walk right into the children's rooms while they were dressing. "Now she must be looking over her costumes to see which one to wear." Moon Orchid pulled out a dress. "This is nice," she suggested. "Look at all the colors."

"No, Aunt. That's the kind of dress for a party. I'm going to school now."

"Oh, she's going to school now. She's choosing a plain blue dress. She's picking up her comb and brush and shoes, and she's going to lock herself up in the bathroom. They dress in bathrooms here." She pressed her ear against the door. "She's brushing her teeth. Now she's coming out of the bathroom. She's wearing the blue dress and a white sweater. She's combed her hair and washed her face. She looks in the refrigerator and is arranging things between slices of bread. She's putting an orange and cookies in a bag. Today she's taking her green book and her blue book. And tablets and pencils. Do you take a dictionary?" Moon Orchid asked.

"No," said the child, rolling her eyeballs up and exhaling loudly. "We have dictionaries at school," she added before going out the door.

"They have dictionaries at school," said Moon Orchid, thinking this over. "She knows 'dictionary.'" Moon Orchid stood at the window peeping. "Now she's shutting the gate. She strides along like an Englishman."

The child married to a husband who did not speak Chinese translated for him, "Now she's saying that I'm taking a machine off the shelf and that I'm attaching two metal spiders to it. And she's saying the spiders are spinning with legs intertwined and beating the eggs electrically. Now she says I'm hunting for something in the refrigerator and—ha!—I've found it. I'm taking out butter—'cow oil.' 'They eat a lot of cow oil,' she's saying."

"She's driving me nuts!" the children told each other in English.

At the laundry Moon Orchid hovered so close that there was barely room between her and the hot presses. "Now the index fingers of both hands press the buttons, and—ka-lump—the press comes down. But one finger on a button will release it—ssssss—the steam lets loose. Sssst—the water squirts." She could describe it so well, you would think she could do it. She wasn't as hard to take at the laundry as at home, though. She could not endure the heat, and after a while she had to go out on the sidewalk and sit on her apple crate. When they were younger the children used to sit out there too during their breaks. They played house and store and library, their orange and apple crates in a row. Passers-by and customers gave them money. But now they were older, they stayed inside or went for walks. They were ashamed of sitting on the sidewalk, people mistaking them for beggars. "Dance for me," the ghosts would say before handing them a nickel. "Sing a Chinese song." And before they got old enough to know better, they'd dance and they'd sing. Moon Orchid sat out there by herself.

Whenever Brave Orchid thought of it, which was everyday, she said, "Are you ready to go see your husband and claim what is yours?"

"Not today, but soon," Moon Orchid would reply.

But one day in the middle of summer, Moon Orchid's daughter said, "I have to return to my family. I promised my husband and children I'd only be gone a few weeks. I should return this week." Moon Orchid's daughter lived in Los Angeles.

"Good!" Brave Orchid exclaimed. "We'll all go to Los Angeles. You return to your husband, and your mother returns to hers. We only have to make one trip."

"You ought to leave the poor man alone," said Brave Orchid's husband. "Leave him out of women's business."

"When your father lived in China," Brave Orchid told the children, "he refused to eat pastries because he didn't want to eat the dirt the women kneaded from between their fingers."

"But I'm happy here with you and all your children," Moon Orchid said. "I want to see how this girl's sewing turns out. I want to see your son come back from Vietnam. I want to see if this one gets good grades. There's so much to do."

"We're leaving on Friday," said Brave Orchid. "I'm going to escort you, and you will arrive safely."

On Friday Brave Orchid put on her dress-up clothes, which she wore only a few times during the year. Moon Orchid wore the same kind of clothes she wore every day and was dressed up. Brave Orchid told her oldest son he had to drive. He drove, and the two old ladies and the niece sat in the back seat.

They set out at gray dawn, driving between the grape trees, which hunched like dwarfs in the fields. Gnomes in serrated outfits that blew in the morning wind came out of the earth, came up in rows and columns. Everybody was only half awake. "A long time ago," began Brave Orchid, "the emperors had four wives, one at each point of the compass, and they lived in four palaces. The Empress of the West would connive for power, but the Empress of the East was good and kind and full of light. You are the Empress of the East, and the Empress of the West has imprisoned the Earth's Emperor in the Western Palace. And you, the good Empress of the East, come out of the dawn to invade her land and free the Emperor. You must break the strong spell she has cast on him that has lost him the East."

Brave Orchid gave her sister last-minute advice for five hundred miles. All her possessions had been packed into the trunk.

"Shall we go into your house together," asked Brave Orchid, "or do you want to go by yourself?"

"You've got to come with me. I don't know what I would say."

"I think it would be dramatic for you to go by yourself. He opens the door. And there you are—alive and standing on the porch with all your luggage. 'Remember me?' you say. Call him by his own name. He'll faint with shock. Maybe he'll say, 'No. Go away.' But you march right in. You push him aside and go in. Then you sit down in the most important chair, and you take off your shoes because you belong."

"Don't you think he'll welcome me?"

"She certainly wasn't very imaginative," thought Brave Orchid.

"It's against the law to have two wives in this country," said Moon Orchid. "I read that in the newspaper."

"But it's probably against the law in Singapore too. Yet our brother has two, and his sons have two each. The law doesn't matter."

"I'm scared. Oh, let's turn back. I don't want to see him. Suppose he throws me out? Oh, he will. He'll throw me out. And he'll have a right to throw me out, coming here, disturbing him, not waiting for him to invite me. Don't leave me by myself. You can talk louder than I can."

"Yes, coming with you would be exciting. I can charge through the door and say, 'Where is your wife?' And he'll answer, 'Why, she's right here.' And I'll say, 'This isn't your wife. Where is Moon Orchid? I've come to see her. I'm her first sister, and I've come to see that she is being well taken care of.' Then I accuse him of murderous things; I'd have him arrested—and you pop up to his rescue. Or I can take a look at his wife, and I say, 'Moon Orchid, how young you've gotten.' And he'll say, 'This isn't Moon Orchid.' And you come in and say, 'No. I am.' If nobody's home, we'll climb in a window. When they get back we'll be at home; you the hostess, and I your guest. You'll be serving me cookies and coffee. And when he comes in I'll say, 'Well, I see your husband is home. Thank you so much for the visit.' And you say, 'Come again anytime.' Don't make violence. Be routine."

Sometimes Moon Orchid got into the mood. "Maybe I could be folding towels when he comes in. He'll think I'm so clever. I'll get to them before his wife does." But the further they came down the great central valley—green fields changing to fields of cotton on dry, brown stalks, first a stray bush here and there, then thick—the more Moon Orchid wanted to turn back. "No. I can't go through with this." She tapped her nephew on the shoulder. "Please turn

back. Oh, you must turn the car around. I should be returning to China. I shouldn't be here at all. Let's go back. Do
you understand me?"

"Don't go back," Brave Orchid ordered her son. "Keep
going. She can't back out now."

"What do you want me to do? Make up your minds,"
said the son, who was getting impatient.

"Keep going," said Brave Orchid. "She's come this far,
and we can't waste all this driving. Besides, we have to
take your cousin back to her own house in Los Angeles. We
have to drive to Los Angeles anyway."

"Can I go inside and meet my grandchildren?"

"Yes," said her daughter.

"We'll see them after you straighten out things with
your husband," said Brave Orchid.

"What if he hits me?"

"I'll hit *him*. I'll protect you. I'll hit him back. The two
of us will knock him down and make him listen." Brave
Orchid chuckled as if she were looking forward to a fight.
But when she saw how terrified Moon Orchid was, she said,
"It won't come to a fight. You mustn't start imagining
things. We'll simply walk up to the door. If he answers,
you'll say, 'I have decided to come live with you in the
Beautiful Nation.' If *she* answers the door, you'll say, 'You
must be Little Wife. I am Big Wife.' Why, you could even
be generous. 'I'd like to see our husband, please,' you say.
I brought my wig," said Brave Orchid. "Why don't you
disguise yourself as a beautiful lady? I brought lipstick and
powder too. And at some dramatic point, you pull off the
wig and say, 'I am Moon Orchid.' "

"That is a terrible thing to do. I'd be so scared. I am so
scared."

"I want to be dropped off at my house first," said the
niece. "I told my family I'd be home to make lunch."

"All right," said Brave Orchid, who had tried to talk
her niece into confronting her father five years ago, but all
she had done was write him a letter telling him she was in

Los Angeles. He could visit her, or she could visit him if he wanted to see her, she had suggested. But he had not wanted to see her.

When the car stopped in front of her daughter's house, Moon Orchid asked, "May I get out to meet my grandchildren?"

"I told you no," said Brave Orchid. "If you do that you'll stay here, and it'll take us weeks to get up our courage again. Let's save your grandchildren as a reward. You take care of this other business, and you can play with your grandchildren without worry. Besides, you have some children to meet."

"Grandchildren are more wonderful than children."

After they left the niece's suburb, the son drove them to the address his mother had given him, which turned out to be a skyscraper in downtown Los Angeles.

"Don't park in front," said his mother. "Find a side street. We've got to take him by surprise. We mustn't let him spot us ahead of time. We have to catch the first look on his face."

"Yes, I think I would like to see the look on his face."

Brave Orchid's son drove up and down the side streets until he found a parking space that could not be seen from the office building.

"You have to compose yourself," said Brave Orchid to her sister. "You must be calm as you walk in. Oh, this is most dramatic—in broad daylight and in the middle of the city. We'll sit here for a while and look at his building."

"Does he own that whole building?"

"I don't know. Maybe so."

"Oh, I can't move. My knees are shaking so much I won't be able to walk. He must have servants and workers in there, and they'll stare at me. I can't bear it."

Brave Orchid felt a tiredness drag her down. She had to baby everyone. The traffic was rushing, Los Angeles noon-hot, and she suddenly felt carsick. No trees. No birds. Only city. "It must be the long drive," she thought. They had not eaten lunch, and the sitting had tired her out. Movement would strengthen her; she needed movement. "I want you to stay here with your aunt while I scout that building," she instructed her son. "When I come back, we'll work out a plan." She walked around the block. Indeed, she felt that her feet stepping on the earth, even when the earth was covered with concrete, gained strength from it. She breathed health from the air, though it was full of gasoline fumes. The bottom floor of the building housed several stores. She looked at the clothes and jewelry on display, picking out some for Moon Orchid to have when she came into her rightful place.

Brave Orchid rushed along beside her reflection in the glass. She used to be young and fast; she was still fast and felt young. It was mirrors, not aches and pains, that turned a person old, everywhere white hairs and wrinkles. Young people felt pain.

The building was a fine one; the lobby was chrome and glass, with ashtray stands and plastic couches arranged in semicircles. She waited for the elevator to fill before she got in, not wanting to operate a new machine by herself. Once on the sixth floor she searched alertly for the number in her address book.

How clean his building was. The rest rooms were locked, and there were square overhead lights. No windows, though. She did not like the quiet corridors with carpets but no windows. They felt like tunnels. He must be very wealthy. Good. It would serve a rich man right to be humbled. She found the door with his number on it; there was also American lettering on the glass. Apparently this was his business office. She hadn't thought of the possibility of catching him at his job. Good thing she had decided to scout. If they had arrived at his house, they would not have found him. Then they would have had to deal with *her*. And she would have phoned him, spoiled the surprise, and gotten him on her side. Brave Orchid knew how the little wives maneuvered; her father had had two little wives.

She entered the office, glad that it was a public place

and she needn't knock. A roomful of men and women looked up from their magazines. She could tell by their eagerness for change that this was a waiting room. Behind a sliding glass partition sat a young woman in a modern nurse's uniform, not a white one, but a light blue pantsuit with white trim. She sat before an elegant telephone and an electric typewriter. The wallpaper in her cubicle was like aluminum foil, a metallic background for a tall black frame around white paint with dashes of red. The wall of the waiting room was covered with burlap, and there were plants in wooden tubs. It was an expensive waiting room. Brave Orchid approved. The patients looked well dressed, not sickly and poor.

"Hello. May I help you?" said the receptionist, parting the glass. Brave Orchid hesitated, and the receptionist took this to mean that she could not speak English. "Just a moment," she said, and went into an inner room. She brought back another woman, who wore a similar uniform except that it was pink trimmed in white. This woman's hair was gathered up into a bunch of curls at the back of her head; some of the curls were fake. She wore round glasses and false eyelashes, which gave her an American look. "Have you an appointment?" she asked in poor Chinese; she spoke less like a Chinese than Brave Orchid's children. "My husband, the doctor, usually does not take drop-in patients," she said. "We're booked up for about a month." Brave Orchid stared at her pink-painted fingernails gesticulating, and thought she probably would not have given out so much information if she weren't so clumsy with language.

"I have the flu," Brave Orchid said.

"Perhaps we can give you the name of another doctor," said this woman, who was her sister-in-law. "This doctor is a brain surgeon and doesn't work with flu." Actually she said, "This doctor cuts brains," a child making up the words as she went along. She wore pink lipstick and had blue eyelids like the ghosts.

Brave Orchid, who had been a surgeon too, thought that her brother-in-law must be a clever man. She herself could not practice openly in the United States because the training here was so different and because she could never learn English. He was smart enough to learn ghost ways. She would have to be clever to outwit him. She needed to retreat and plan some more. "Oh, well, I'll go to another doctor, then," she said, and left.

She needed a new plan to get her sister and brother-in-law together. This nurse-wife was so young, and the office was so rich with wood, paintings, and fancy telephones, that Brave Orchid knew it wasn't because he couldn't get the fare together that he hadn't sent for his old wife. He had abandoned her for this modern, heartless girl. Brave Orchid wondered if the girl knew that her husband had a Chinese wife. Perhaps she should ask her.

But no, she mustn't spoil the surprise by giving any hints. She had to get away before he came out into the corridor, perhaps to go to one of the locked rest rooms. As she walked back to her sister, she noted corners and passageways, broom closets, other offices—ambush spots. Her sister could crouch behind a drinking fountain and wait for him to get thirsty. Waylay him.

"I met his second wife," she said, opening the car door.

"What's she like?" asked Moon Orchid. "Is she pretty?"

"She's very pretty and very young; just a girl. She's his nurse. He's a doctor like me. What a terrible, faithless man. You'll have to scold him for years, but first you need to sit up straight. Use my powder. Be as pretty as you can. Otherwise you won't be able to compete. You do have one advantage, however. Notice he has her be his worker. She is like a servant, so you have room to be the wife. She works at the office; you work at the house. That's almost as good as having two houses. On the other hand, a man's real partner is the hardest worker. You couldn't learn nursing, could you? No, I guess not. It's almost as difficult as doing laundry. What a petty man he turned out to be, giving up responsibility for a pretty face." Brave Orchid reached for the door handle. "Are you ready?"

"For what?"

"To go up there, of course. We're at his office, and I think we ought to be very direct. There aren't any trees to hide you, no grass to soften your steps. So, you walk right into his office. You make an announcement to the patients and the fancy nurses. You say, 'I am the doctor's wife. I'm going to see my husband.' Then you step to the inner door and enter. Don't knock on any doors. Don't listen if the minor wife talks to you. You walk past her without changing pace. When you see him, you say, 'Surprise!' You say, 'Who is that woman out there? She claims to be your wife.' That will give him a chance to deny her on the spot."

"Oh, I'm so scared. I can't move. I can't do that in front of all those people—like a stage show. I won't be able to talk." And sure enough, her voice was fading into a whisper. She was shivering and small in the corner of the seat.

"So. A new plan, then," said Brave Orchid, looking at her son, who had his forehead on the steering wheel. "You, she said. "I want you to go up to his office and tell your uncle that there has been an accident out in the street. A woman's leg has been broken, and she's crying in pain. He'll have to come. You bring him to the car."

"Mother."

"Mm," mused Brave Orchid. "Maybe we ought to put your aunt in the middle of the street, and she can lie down with her leg bent under her." But Moon Orchid kept shaking her head in trembling no's.

"Why don't you push her down in the intersection and pour ketchup on her? I'll run over her a little bit," said her son.

"Stop being silly," she said. "You Americans don't take life seriously."

"Mother, this is ridiculous. This whole thing is ridiculous."

"Go. Do what I tell you," she said.

"I think your schemes will be useless, Mother."

"What do you know about Chinese business?" she said. "Do as I say."

"Don't let him bring the nurse," said Moon Orchid.

"Don't you want to see what she looks like?" asked Brave Orchid. "Then you'll know what he's giving up for you."

"No. No. She's none of my business. She's unimportant."

"Speak in English," Brave Orchid told her son. "Then he'll feel he has to come with you."

She pushed her son out of the car. "I don't want to do this," he said.

"You'll ruin your aunt's life if you don't. You can't understand business begun in China. Just do what I say. Go."

Slamming the car door behind him, he left.

Moon Orchid was groaning now and holding her stomach. "Straighten up," said Brave Orchid. "He'll be here any moment." But this only made Moon Orchid groan louder, and tears seeped out between her closed eyelids.

"You want a husband, don't you?" said Brave Orchid. "If you don't claim him now, you'll never have a husband. Stop crying," she ordered. "Do you want him to see you with your eyes and nose swollen when that young so-called wife wears lipstick and nail polish like a movie star?"

Moon Orchid managed to sit upright, but she seemed stiff and frozen.

"You're just tired from the ride. Put some blood into your cheeks," Brave Orchid said, and pinched her sister's withered face. She held her sister's elbow and slapped the inside of her arm. If she had had time, she would have hit until the black and red dots broke out on the skin; that was the tiredness coming out. As she hit, she kept an eye on the rearview mirror. She saw her son come running, his uncle after him with a black bag in his hand. "Faster. Faster," her son was saying. He opened the car door. "Here she is," he said to his uncle. "I'll see you later." And he ran on down the street.

The two old ladies saw a man, authoritative in his dark

western suit, start to fill the front of the car. He had black
hair and no wrinkles. He looked and smelled like an American. Suddenly the two women remembered that in China
families married young boys to older girls, who baby-sat
their husbands their whole lives. Either that or, in this
ghost country, a man could somehow keep his youth.

"Where's the accident?" he said in Chinese. "What is
this? You don't have a broken leg."

Neither woman spoke. Brave Orchid held her words
back. She would not let herself interfere with this meeting
after long absence.

"What is it?" he asked. "What's wrong?" These women
had such awful faces. "What is it, Grandmothers?"

"Grandmother?" Brave Orchid shouted. "This is your
wife. I am your sister-in-law."

Moon Orchid started to whimper. Her husband looked
at her. And recognized her. "You," he said. "What are you
doing here?"

But all she did was open and shut her mouth without
any words coming out.

"Why are you here?" he asked, eyes wide. Moon Orchid covered her face with one hand and motioned no with
the other.

Brave Orchid could not keep silent. Obviously he was
not glad to see his wife. "I sent for her," she burst out. "I
got her name on the Red Cross list, and I sent her the plane
ticket. I wrote her every day and gave her the heart to
come. I told her how welcome she would be, how her family
would welcome her, how her husband would welcome her.
I did what you, the husband, had time to do in these last
thirty years."

He looked directly at Moon Orchid the way the savages
looked, looking for lies. "What do you want?" he asked.
She shrank from his stare; it silenced her crying.

"You weren't supposed to come here," he said, the front
seat a barrier against the two women over whom a spell
of old age had been cast. "It's a mistake for you to be here.

You can't belong. You don't have the hardness for this country. I have a new life."

"What about me?" whispered Moon Orchid.

"Good," thought Brave Orchid. "Well said. Said with no guile."

"I have a new wife," said the man.

"She's only your second wife," said Brave Orchid. "This is your real wife."

"In this country a man may have just one wife."

"So you'll get rid of that creature in your office?" asked Brave Orchid.

He looked at Moon Orchid. Again the rude American eyes. "You go live with your daughter. I'll mail you the money I've always sent you. I could get arrested if the Americans knew about you. I'm living like an American." He talked like a child born here.

"How could you ruin her old age?" said Brave Orchid.

"She has had food. She has had servants. Her daughter went to college. There wasn't anything she thought of that she couldn't buy. I have been a good husband."

"You made her live like a widow."

"That's not true. Obviously the villagers haven't stoned her. She's not wearing mourning. The family didn't send her away to work. Look at her. She'd never fit into an American household. I have important American guests who come inside my house to eat." He turned to Moon Orchid, "You can't talk to them. You can barely talk to me."

Moon Orchid was so ashamed, she held her hands over her face. She wished she could also hide her dappled hands. Her husband looked like one of the ghosts passing the car windows, and she must look like a ghost from China. They had indeed entered the land of ghosts, and they had become ghosts.

"Do you want her to go back to China then?" Brave Orchid was asking.

"I wouldn't wish that on anyone. She may stay, but I do not want her in my house. She has to live with you or with her daughter, and I don't want either of you coming here anymore."

Suddenly his nurse was tapping on the glass. So quickly that they might have missed it, he gestured to the old women, holding a finger to his mouth for just a moment: he had never told his American wife that he had a wife in China, and they mustn't tell her either.

"What's happening?" she asked. "Do you need help? The appointments are piling up."

"No. No," he said. "This woman fainted in the street. I'll be up soon."

They spoke to each other in English.

The two old women did not call out to the young woman. Soon she left. "I'm leaving too now," said the husband.

"Why didn't you write to tell her once and for all you weren't coming back and you weren't sending for her?" Brave Orchid asked.

"I don't know," he said. "It's as if I had turned into a different person. The new life around me was so complete; it pulled me away. You became people in a book I had read a long time ago."

"The least you can do," said Brave Orchid, "is invite us to lunch. Aren't you inviting us to lunch? Don't you owe us a lunch? At a good restaurant?" She would not let him off easily.

So he bought them lunch, and when Brave Orchid's son came back to the car, he had to wait for them.

Moon Orchid was driven back to her daughter's house, but though she lived in Los Angeles, she never saw her husband again. "Oh, well," said Brave Orchid. "We're all under the same sky and walk the same earth; we're alive together during the same moment." Brave Orchid and her son drove back north, Brave Orchid sitting in the back seat the whole way.

Several months went by with no letter from Moon Orchid. When she had lived in China and in Hong Kong, she had written every other week. At last Brave Orchid telephoned long distance to find out what was happening. "I can't talk now," Moon Orchid whispered. "They're listening. Hang up quickly before they trace you." Moon Orchid hung up on Brave Orchid before the minutes she had paid for expired.

That week a letter came from the niece saying that Moon Orchid had become afraid. Moon Orchid said that she had overheard Mexican ghosts plotting on her life. She had been creeping along the baseboards and peeping out windows. Then she had asked her daughter to help her find an apartment at the other end of Los Angeles, where she was now hiding. Her daughter visited her every day, but Moon Orchid kept telling her, "Don't come see me because the Mexican ghosts will follow you to my new hiding place. They're watching your house."

Brave Orchid phoned her niece and told her to send her mother north immediately, where there were no Mexicans, she said. "This fear is an illness," she told her niece. "I will cure her." ("Long ago," she explained to her children, "when the emperors had four wives, the wife who lost in battle was sent to the Northern Palace. Her feet would sink little prints into the snow.")

Brave Orchid sat on a bench at the Greyhound station to wait for her sister. Her children had not come with her because the bus station was only a five-block walk from the house. Her brown paper shopping bag against her, she dozed under the fluorescent lights until her sister's bus pulled into the terminal. Moon Orchid stood blinking on the stairs, hanging tightly to the railing for old people. Brave Orchid felt the tears break inside her chest for the old feet that stepped one at a time onto the cold Greyhound cement. Her sister's skin hung loose, like a hollowed frog's, as if she had shrunken inside it. Her clothes bagged, not fitting sharply anymore. "I'm in disguise," she said. Brave Orchid put her arms around her sister to give her body warmth. She held her hand along the walk home, just as they had held hands when they were girls.

The house was more crowded than ever, though some of the children had gone away to school; the jade trees were inside for the winter. Along walls and on top of tables, jade trees, whose trunks were as thick as ankles, stood stoutly, green now and without the pink skin the sun gave them in the spring.

"I am so afraid," said Moon Orchid.

"There is no one after you," said Brave Orchid. "No Mexicans."

"I saw some in the Greyhound station," said Moon Orchid.

"No. No, those were Filipinos." She held her sister's earlobes and began the healing chant for being unafraid. "There are no Mexicans after you," she said.

"I know. I got away from them by escaping on the bus."

"Yes, you escaped on the bus with the mark of the dog on it."

In the evening, when Moon Orchid seemed quieter, her sister probed into the cause of this trouble.

"What made you think anyone was after you?"

"I heard them talking about me. I snuck up on them and heard them."

"But you don't understand Mexican words."

"They were speaking English."

"You don't understand English words."

"This time, miraculously, I understood. I decoded their speech. I penetrated the words and understood what was happening inside."

Brave Orchid tweaked her sister's ears for hours, chanting her new address to her, telling her how much she loved her and how much her daughter and nephews and nieces loved her, and her brother-in-law loved her. "I won't let anything happen to you. I won't let you travel again. You're home. Stay home. Don't be afraid." Tears fell from Brave Orchid's eyes. She had whisked her sister across the ocean by jet and then made her scurry up and down the Pacific coast, back and forth across Los Angeles. Moon Orchid had misplaced herself, her spirit (her "attention," Brave Orchid called it) scattered all over the world. Brave Orchid held her sister's head as she pulled on her earlobe. She would make it up to her. For moments an attentiveness would return to Moon Orchid's face. Brave Orchid rubbed the slender hands, blew on the fingers, tried to stoke up the flickerings. She stayed home from the laundry day after day. She threw out the Thorazine and vitamin B that a doctor in Los Angeles had prescribed. She made Moon Orchid sit in the kitchen sun while she picked over the herbs in cupboards and basement and the fresh plants that grew in the winter garden. Brave Orchid chose the gentlest plants and made medicines and foods like those they had eaten in their village.

At night she moved from her own bedroom and slept beside Moon Orchid. "Don't be afraid to sleep," she said. "Rest. I'll be here beside you. I'll help your spirit find the place to come back to. I'll call it for you; you go to sleep." Brave Orchid stayed awake watching until dawn.

Moon Orchid still described aloud her nieces' and nephews' doings, but now in a monotone, and she no longer interrupted herself to ask questions. She would not go outside, even into the yard. "Why, she's mad," Brave Orchid's husband said when she was asleep.

Brave Orchid held her hand when she appeared vague. "Don't go away, Little Sister. Don't go any further. Come back to us." If Moon Orchid fell asleep on the sofa, Brave Orchid sat up through the night, sometimes dozing in a chair. When Moon Orchid fell asleep in the middle of the bed, Brave Orchid made a place for herself at the foot. She would anchor her sister to this earth.

But each day Moon Orchid slipped further away. She said that the Mexicans had traced her to this house. That was the day she shut the drapes and blinds and locked the doors. She sidled along the walls to peep outside. Brave Orchid told her husband that he must humor his sister-in-law. It was right to shut the windows; it kept her spirit from leaking away. Then Moon Orchid went about the house turning off the lights like during air raids. The house became gloomy; no air, no light. This was very tricky, the darkness a wide way for going as well as coming back. Sometimes Brave Orchid would switch on the lights, calling her sister's name all the while. Brave Orchid's husband installed an air conditioner.

The children locked themselves up in their bedrooms, in the storeroom and basement, where they turned on the lights. Their aunt would come knocking on the doors and say, "Are you all right in there?"

"Yes, Aunt, we're all right."

"Beware," she'd warn. "Beware. Turn off your lights so you won't be found. Turn off the lights before they come for us."

The children hung blankets over the cracks in the doorjambs; they stuffed clothes along the bottoms of doors. "Chinese people are very weird," they told one another.

Next Moon Orchid removed all the photographs, except for those of the grandmother and grandfather, from the shelves, dressers, and walls. She gathered up the family albums. "Hide these," she whispered to Brave Orchid. "Hide these. When they find me, I don't want them to trace the rest of the family. They use photographs to trace you." Brave Orchid wrapped the pictures and the albums in flannel. "I'll carry these far away where no one will find us," she said. When Moon Orchid wasn't looking, she put them at the bottom of a storage box in the basement. She piled old clothes and old shoes on top. "If they come for me," Moon Orchid said, "everyone will be safe."

"We're all safe," said Brave Orchid.

The next odd thing Moon Orchid did was to cry whenever anyone left the house. She held on to them, pulled at their clothes, begged them not to go. The children and Brave Orchid's husband had to sneak out. "Don't let them go," pleaded Moon Orchid. "They will never come back."

"They will come back. Wait and see. I promise you.

Watch for them. Don't watch for Mexicans. This one will be home at 3:30. This one at 5:00. Remember who left now. You'll see."

"We'll never see that one again," Moon Orchid wept.

At 3:30 Brave Orchid would remind her, "See? It's 3:30; sure enough, here he comes." ("You children come home right after school. Don't you dare stop for a moment. No candy store. No comic book store. Do you hear?")

But Moon Orchid did not remember. "Who is this?" she'd ask. "Are you going to stay with us? Don't go out tonight. Don't leave in the morning."

She whispered to Brave Orchid that the reason the family must not go out was that "they" would take us in airplanes and fly us to Washington, D.C., where they'd turn us into ashes. Then they'd drop the ashes in the wind, leaving no evidence.

Brave Orchid saw that all variety had gone from her sister. She was indeed mad. "The difference between mad people and sane people," Brave Orchid explained to the children, "is that sane people have variety when they talk-story. Mad people have only one story that they talk over and over."

Every morning Moon Orchid stood by the front door whispering, whispering. "Don't go. The planes. Ashes. Washington, D.C. Ashes." Then, when a child managed to leave, she said, "That's the last time we'll see him again. They'll get him. They'll turn him into ashes."

And so Brave Orchid gave up. She was housing a mad sister who cursed the mornings for her children, the one in Vietnam too. Their aunt was saying terrible things when they needed blessing. Perhaps Moon Orchid had already left this mad old body, and it was a ghost bad-mouthing her children. Brave Orchid finally called her niece, who put Moon Orchid in a California state mental asylum. Then Brave Orchid opened up the windows and let the air and light come into the house again. She moved back into the bedroom with her husband. The children took the blankets and sheets down from the doorjambs and came back into the living room.

Brave Orchid visited her sister twice. Moon Orchid was thinner each time, shrunken to bone. But, surprisingly, she was happy and had made up a new story. She pranced like a child. "Oh, Sister, I am so happy here. No one ever leaves. Isn't that wonderful? We are all women here. Come. I want you to meet my daughters." She introduced Brave Orchid to each inmate in the ward—her daughters. She was especially proud of the pregnant ones. "My dear pregnant daughters." She touched the women on the head, straightened collars, tucked blankets. "How are you today, dear daughter?" "And, you know," she said to Brave Orchid, "we understand one another here. We speak the same language, the very same. They understand me, and I understand them." Sure enough, the women smiled back at her and reached out to touch her as she went by. She had a new story, and yet she slipped entirely away, not waking up one morning.

Brave Orchid told her children they must help her keep their father from marrying another woman because she didn't think she could take it any better than her sister had. If he brought another woman into the house, they were to gang up on her and play tricks on her, hit her, and trip her when she was carrying hot oil until she ran away. "I am almost seventy years old," said the father, "and haven't taken a second wife, and don't plan to now." Brave Orchid's daughters decided fiercely that they would never let men be unfaithful to them. All her children made up their minds to major in science or mathematics.

A Song

for a

Barbarian

Reed Pipe

What my brother actually said was, "I drove Mom and Second Aunt to Los Angeles to see Aunt's husband who's got the other wife."

"Did she hit him? What did she say? What did he say?"

"Nothing much. Mom did all the talking."

"What did she say?"

"She said he'd better take them to lunch at least."

"Which wife did he sit next to? What did they eat?"

"I didn't go. The other wife didn't either. He motioned us not to tell."

"I would've told. If I was his wife, I would've told. I would've gone to lunch and kept my ears open."

"Ah, you know they don't talk when they eat."

"What else did Mom say?"

"I don't remember. I pretended a pedestrian broke her leg so he would come."

"There must've been more. Didn't Aunt get in one nasty word? She must've said something."

"No, I don't think she said anything. I don't remember her saying one thing."

In fact, it wasn't me my brother told about going to Los Angeles; one of my sisters told me what he'd told her. His version of the story may be better than mine because of its bareness, not twisted into designs. The hearer can carry it tucked away without it taking up much room. Long ago in China, knot-makers tied string into buttons and frogs, and rope into bell pulls. There was one knot so complicated that it blinded the knot-maker. Finally an emperor outlawed this cruel knot, and the nobles could not order it anymore. If I had lived in China, I would have been an outlaw knot-maker.

Maybe that's why my mother cut my tongue. She pushed

my tongue up and sliced the frenum. Or maybe she snipped it with a pair of nail scissors. I don't remember her doing it, only her telling me about it, but all during childhood I felt sorry for the baby whose mother waited with scissors or knife in hand for it to cry—and then, when its mouth was wide open like a baby bird's, cut. The Chinese say "a ready tongue is an evil."

I used to curl up my tongue in front of the mirror and tauten my frenum into a white line, itself as thin as a razor blade. I saw no scars in my mouth. I thought perhaps I had had two frena, and she had cut one. I made other children open their mouths so I could compare theirs to mine. I saw perfect pink membranes stretching into precise edges that looked easy enough to cut. Sometimes I felt very proud that my mother committed such a powerful act upon me. At other times I was terrified—the first thing my mother did when she saw me was to cut my tongue.

"Why did you do that to me, Mother?"

"I told you."

"Tell me again."

"I cut it so that you would not be tongue-tied. Your tongue would be able to move in any language. You'll be able to speak languages that are completely different from one another. You'll be able to pronounce anything. Your frenum looked too tight to do those things, so I cut it."

"But isn't 'a ready tongue an evil'?"

"Things are different in this ghost country."

"Did it hurt me? Did I cry and bleed?"

"I don't remember. Probably."

She didn't cut the other children's. When I asked cousins and other Chinese children whether their mothers had cut their tongues loose, they said, "What?"

"Why didn't you cut my brothers' and sisters' tongues?"

"They didn't need it."

"Why not? Were theirs longer than mine?"

"Why don't you quit blabbering and get to work?"

If my mother was not lying she should have cut more,

scraped away the rest of the frenum skin, because I have a terrible time talking. Or she should not have cut at all, tampering with my speech. When I went to kindergarten and had to speak English for the first time, I became silent. A dumbness—a shame—still cracks my voice in two, even when I want to say "hello" casually, or ask an easy question in front of the check-out counter, or ask directions of a bus driver. I stand frozen, or I hold up the line with the complete, grammatical sentence that comes squeaking out at impossible length. "What did you say?" says the cab driver, or "Speak up," so I have to perform again, only weaker the second time. A telephone call makes my throat bleed and takes up that day's courage. It spoils my day with self-disgust when I hear my broken voice come skittering out into the open. It makes people wince to hear it. I'm getting better, though. Recently I asked the postman for special-issue stamps; I've waited since childhood for postmen to give me some of their own accord. I am making progress, a little every day.

My silence was thickest—total—during the three years that I covered my school paintings with black paint. I painted layers of black over houses and flowers and suns, and when I drew on the blackboard, I put a layer of chalk on top. I was making a stage curtain, and it was the moment before the curtain parted or rose. The teachers called my parents to school, and I saw they had been saving my pictures, curling and cracking, all alike and black. The teachers pointed to the pictures and looked serious, talked seriously too, but my parents did not understand English. ("The parents and teachers of criminals were executed," said my father.) My parents took the pictures home. I spread them out (so black and full of possibilities) and pretended the curtains were swinging open, flying up, one after another, sunlight underneath, mighty operas.

During the first silent year I spoke to no one at school, did not ask before going to the lavatory, and flunked kindergarten. My sister also said nothing for three years, silent in the playground and silent at lunch. There were other quiet Chinese girls not of our family, but most of them got over it sooner than we did. I enjoyed the silence. At first it did not occur to me I was supposed to talk or to pass kindergarten. I talked at home and to one or two of the Chinese kids in class. I made motions and even made some jokes. I drank out of a toy saucer when the water spilled out of the cup, and everybody laughed, pointing at me, so I did it some more. I didn't know that Americans don't drink out of saucers.

I liked the Negro students (Black Ghosts) best because they laughed the loudest and talked to me as if I were a daring talker too. One of the Negro girls had her mother coil braids over her ears Shanghai-style like mine; we were Shanghai twins except that she was covered with black like my paintings. Two Negro kids enrolled in Chinese school, and the teachers gave them Chinese names. Some Negro kids walked me to school and home, protecting me from the Japanese kids, who hit me and chased me and stuck gum in my ears. The Japanese kids were noisy and tough. They appeared one day in kindergarten, released from concentration camp, which was a tic-tac-toe mark, like barbed wire, on the map.

It was when I found out I had to talk that school became a misery, that the silence became a misery. I did not speak and felt bad each time that I did not speak. I read aloud in first grade, though, and heard the barest whisper with little squeaks come out of my throat. "Louder," said the teacher, who scared the voice away again. The other Chinese girls did not talk either, so I knew the silence had to do with being a Chinese girl.

Reading out loud was easier than speaking because we did not have to make up what to say, but I stopped often, and the teacher would think I'd gone quiet again. I could not understand "I." The Chinese "I" has seven strokes, intricacies. How could the American "I," assuredly wearing a hat like the Chinese, have only three strokes, the middle so straight? Was it out of politeness that this writer left off strokes the way a Chinese has to write her own name small and crooked? No, it was not politeness; "I" is a capital and "you" is lower-case. I stared at that middle line and waited so long for its black center to resolve into tight strokes and dots that I forgot to pronounce it. The other troublesome word was "here," no strong consonant to hang on to, and so flat, when "here" is two mountainous ideographs. The teacher, who had already told me every day how to read "I" and "here," put me in the low corner under the stairs again, where the noisy boys usually sat.

When my second grade class did a play, the whole class went to the auditorium except the Chinese girls. The teacher, lovely and Hawaiian, should have understood about us, but instead left us behind in the classroom. Our voices were too soft or nonexistent, and our parents never signed the permission slips anyway. They never signed anything unnecessary. We opened the door a crack and peeked out, but closed it again quickly. One of us (not me) won every spelling bee, though.

I remember telling the Hawaiian teacher, "We Chinese can't sing 'land where our fathers died.' " She argued with me about politics, while I meant because of curses. But how can I have that memory when I couldn't talk? My mother says that we, like the ghosts, have no memories.

After American school, we picked up our cigar boxes, in which we had arranged books, brushes, and an inkbox neatly, and went to Chinese school, from 5:00 to 7:30 P.M. There we chanted together, voices rising and falling, loud and soft, some boys shouting, everybody reading together, reciting together and not alone with one voice. When we had a memorization test, the teacher let each of us come to his desk and say the lesson to him privately, while the rest of the class practiced copying or tracing. Most of the teachers were men. The boys who were so well behaved in the American school played tricks on them and talked back to them. The girls were not mute. They screamed and yelled during recess, when there were no rules; they had fist-fights. Nobody was afraid of children hurting themselves or of children hurting school property. The glass doors to the red and green balconies with the gold joy symbols were left wide open so that we could run out and climb the fire escapes. We played capture-the-flag in the auditorium, where Sun Yat-sen and Chiang Kai-shek's pictures hung at the back of the stage, the Chinese flag on their left and the American flag on their right. We climbed the teak ceremonial chairs and made flying leaps off the stage. One flag headquarters was behind the glass door and the other on stage right. Our feet drummed on the hollow stage. During recess the teachers locked themselves up in their office with the shelves of books, copybooks, inks from China. They drank tea and warmed their hands at a stove. There was no play supervision. At recess we had the school to ourselves, and also we could roam as far as we could go—downtown, Chinatown stores, home—as long as we returned before the bell rang.

At exactly 7:30 the teacher again picked up the brass bell that sat on his desk and swung it over our heads, while we charged down the stairs, our cheering magnified in the stairwell. Nobody had to line up.

Not all of the children who were silent at American school found voice at Chinese school. One new teacher said each of us had to get up and recite in front of the class, who was to listen. My sister and I had memorized the lesson perfectly. We said it to each other at home, one chanting, one listening. The teacher called on my sister to recite first. It was the first time a teacher had called on the second-born to go first. My sister was scared. She glanced at me and looked away; I looked down at my desk. I hoped that she could do it because if she could, then I would have to. She opened her mouth and a voice came out that wasn't a whisper, but it wasn't a proper voice either. I hoped that she would not cry, fear breaking up her voice like twigs underfoot. She sounded as if she were trying to sing though weeping and strangling. She did not pause or stop to end the embarrassment. She kept going until she said the last word, and then she sat down. When it was my turn, the same voice came out, a crippled animal running on broken legs. You could hear splinters in my voice, bones rubbing jagged against one another. I was loud, though. I was glad I didn't whisper. There was one little girl who whispered.

You can't entrust your voice to the Chinese, either; they want to capture your voice for their own use. They want to fix up your tongue to speak for them. "How much less can you sell it for?" we have to say. Talk the Sales Ghosts down. Make them take a loss.

We were working at the laundry when a delivery boy came from the Rexall drugstore around the corner. He had a pale blue box of pills, but nobody was sick. Reading the label we saw that it belonged to another Chinese family, Crazy Mary's family. "Not ours," said my father. He pointed out the name to the Delivery Ghost, who took the pills back. My mother muttered for an hour, and then her anger boiled over. "That ghost! That dead ghost! How dare he come to the wrong house?" She could not concentrate on her marking and pressing. "A mistake! Huh!" I was getting angry myself. She fumed. She made her press crash and hiss. "Revenge. We've got to avenge this wrong on our future, on our health, and on our lives. Nobody's going to sicken my children and get away with it." We brothers and sisters did not look at one another. She would do something awful, something embarrassing. She'd already been hinting that during the next eclipse we slam pot lids together to scare the frog from swallowing the moon. (The word for "eclipse" is *frog-swallowing-the-moon*.) When we had not banged lids at the last eclipse and the shadow kept receding anyway, she'd said, "The villagers must be banging and clanging very loudly back home in China."

("On the other side of the world, they aren't having an eclipse, Mama. That's just a shadow the earth makes when it comes between the moon and the sun."

"You're always believing what those Ghost Teachers tell you. Look at the size of the jaws!")

"Aha!" she yelled. "You! The biggest." She was pointing at me. "You go to the drugstore."

"What do you want me to buy, Mother?" I said.

"Buy nothing. Don't bring one cent. Go and make them stop the curse."

"I don't want to go. I don't know how to do that. There are no such things as curses. They'll think I'm crazy."

"If you don't go, I'm holding you responsible for bringing a plague on this family."

"What am I supposed to do when I get there?" I said, sullen, trapped. "Do I say, 'Your delivery boy made a wrong delivery'?"

"They know he made a wrong delivery. I want you to make them rectify their crime."

I felt sick already. She'd make me swing stinky censers around the counter, at the druggist, at the customers. Throw dog blood on the druggist. I couldn't stand her plans.

"You get reparation candy," she said. "You say, 'You have tainted my house with sick medicine and must remove the curse with sweetness.' He'll understand."

"He didn't do it on purpose. And no, he won't, Mother. They don't understand stuff like that. I won't be able to say it right. He'll call us beggars."

"You just translate." She searched me to make sure I wasn't hiding any money. I was sneaky and bad enough to buy the candy and come back pretending it was a free gift.

"Mymotherseztagimmesomecandy," I said to the druggist. Be cute and small. No one hurts the cute and small.

"What? Speak up. Speak English," he said, big in his white druggist coat.

"Tatatagimme somecandy."

The druggist leaned way over the counter and frowned. "Some free candy," I said. "Sample candy."

"We don't give sample candy, young lady," he said.

"My mother said you have to give us candy. She said that is the way the Chinese do it."

"What?"

"That is the way the Chinese do it."

"Do what?"

"Do things." I felt the weight and immensity of things impossible to explain to the druggist.

"Can I give you some money?" he asked.

"No, we want candy."

He reached into a jar and gave me a handful of lollipops. He gave us candy all year round, year after year, every time we went into the drugstore. When different druggists or clerks waited on us, they also gave us candy. They had talked us over. They gave us Halloween candy in December, Christmas candy around Valentine's day, candy hearts at Easter, and Easter eggs at Halloween. "See?" said our mother. "They understand. You kids just aren't very brave." But I knew they did not understand. They thought we were beggars without a home who lived in back of the laundry. They felt sorry for us. I did not eat their candy. I did not go inside the drugstore or walk past it unless my parents forced me to. Whenever we had a prescription filled, the druggist put candy in the medicine bag. This is what Chinese druggists normally do, except they give raisins. My mother thought she taught the Druggist Ghosts a lesson in good manners (which is the same word as "traditions").

My mouth went permanently crooked with effort, turned down on the left side and straight on the right. How strange that the emigrant villagers are shouters, hollering face to face. My father asks, "Why is it I can hear Chinese from blocks away? Is it that I understand the language? Or is it they talk loud?" They turn the radio up full blast to hear the operas, which do not seem to hurt their ears. And they yell over the singers that wail over the drums, everybody talking at once, big arm gestures, spit flying. You can see the disgust on American faces looking at women like that. It isn't just the loudness. It is the way Chinese sounds, chingchong ugly, to American ears, not beautiful like Japanese sayonara words with the consonants and vowels as regular as Italian. We make guttural peasant

noise and have Ton Duc Thang names you can't remember.
And the Chinese can't hear Americans at all; the language
is too soft and western music unhearable. I've watched a
Chinese audience laugh, visit, talk-story, and holler during
a piano recital, as if the musician could not hear them. A
Chinese-American, somebody's son, was playing Chopin,
which has no punctuation, no cymbals, no gongs. Chinese
piano music is five black keys. Normal Chinese women's
voices are strong and bossy. We American-Chinese girls
had to whisper to make ourselves American-feminine. Apparently we whispered even more softly than the Americans. Once a year the teachers referred my sister and me
to speech therapy, but our voices would straighten out,
unpredictably normal, for the therapists. Some of us gave
up, shook our heads, and said nothing, not one word. Some
of us could not even shake our heads. At times shaking
my head no is more self-assertion than I can manage. Most
of us eventually found some voice, however faltering. We
invented an American-feminine speaking personality, except for that one girl who could not speak up even in Chinese school.

She was a year older than I and was in my class for
twelve years. During all those years she read aloud but
would not talk. Her older sister was usually beside her;
their parents kept the older daughter back to protect the
younger one. They were six and seven years old when they
began school. Although I had flunked kindergarten, I was
the same age as most other students in our class; my parents had probably lied about my age, so I had had a head
start and came out even. My younger sister was in the
class below me; we were normal ages and normally separated. The parents of the quiet girl, on the other hand,
protected both daughters. When it sprinkled, they kept
them home from school. The girls did not work for a living
the way we did. But in other ways we were the same.

We were similar in sports. We held the bat on our
shoulders until we walked to first base. (You got a strike

only when you actually struck at the ball.) Sometimes the pitcher wouldn't bother to throw to us. "Automatic walk," the other children would call, sending us on our way. By fourth or fifth grade, though, some of us would try to hit the ball. "Easy out," the other kids would say. I hit the ball a couple of times. Baseball was nice in that there was a definite spot to run to after hitting the ball. Basketball confused me because when I caught the ball I didn't know whom to throw it to. "Me. Me," the kids would be yelling. "Over here." Suddenly it would occur to me I hadn't memorized which ghosts were on my team and which were on the other. When the kids said, "Automatic walk," the girl who was quieter than I kneeled with one end of the bat in each hand and placed it carefully on the plate. Then she dusted her hands as she walked to first base, where she rubbed her hands softly, fingers spread. She always got tagged out before second base. She would whisper-read but not talk. Her whisper was as soft as if she had no muscles. She seemed to be breathing from a distance. I heard no anger or tension.

I joined in at lunchtime when the other students, the Chinese too, talked about whether or not she was mute, although obviously she was not if she could read aloud. People told how *they* had tried *their* best to be friendly. *They* said hello, but if she refused to answer, well, they didn't see why they had to say hello anymore. She had no friends of her own but followed her sister everywhere, although people and she herself probably thought I was her friend. I also followed her sister about, who was fairly normal. She was almost two years older and read more than anyone else.

I hated the younger sister, the quiet one. I hated her when she was the last chosen for her team and I, the last chosen for my team. I hated her for her China doll hair cut. I hated her at music time for the wheezes that came out of her plastic flute.

One afternoon in the sixth grade (that year I was arrogant with talk, not knowing there were going to be high school dances and college seminars to set me back), I and my little sister and the quiet girl and her big sister stayed late after school for some reason. The cement was cooling, and the tetherball poles made shadows across the gravel. The hooks at the rope ends were clinking against the poles. We shouldn't have been so late; there was laundry work to do and Chinese school to get to by 5:00. The last time we had stayed late, my mother had phoned the police and told them we had been kidnapped by bandits. The radio stations broadcast our descriptions. I had to get home before she did that again. But sometimes if you loitered long enough in the schoolyard, the other children would have gone home and you could play with the equipment before the office took it away. We were chasing one another through the playground and in and out of the basement, where the playroom and lavatory were. During air raid drills (it was during the Korean War, which you knew about because every day the front page of the newspaper printed a map of Korea with the top part red and going up and down like a window shade), we curled up in this basement. Now everyone was gone. The playroom was army green and had nothing in it but a long trough with drinking spigots in rows. Pipes across the ceiling led to the drinking fountains and to the toilets in the next room. When someone flushed you could hear the water and other matter, which the children named, running inside the big pipe above the drinking spigots. There was one playroom for girls next to the girls' lavatory and one playroom for boys next to the boys' lavatory. The stalls were open and the toilets had no lids, by which we knew that ghosts have no sense of shame or privacy.

Inside the playroom the lightbulbs in cages had already been turned off. Daylight came in x-patterns through the caging at the windows. I looked out and, seeing no one in the schoolyard, ran outside to climb the fire escape upside down, hanging on to the metal stairs with fingers and toes.

I did a flip off the fire escape and ran across the schoolyard. The day was a great eye, and it was not paying much attention to me now. I could disappear with the sun; I could turn quickly sideways and slip into a different world. It seemed I could run faster at this time, and by evening I would be able to fly. As the afternoon wore on we could run into the forbidden places—the boys' big yard, the boys' playroom. We could go into the boys' lavatory and look at the urinals. The only time during school hours I had crossed the boys' yard was when a flatbed truck with a giant thing covered with canvas and tied down with ropes had parked across the street. The children had told one another that it was a gorilla in captivity; we couldn't decide whether the sign said "Trail of the Gorilla" or "Trial of the Gorilla." The thing was as big as a house. The teachers couldn't stop us from hysterically rushing to the fence and clinging to the wire mesh. Now I ran across the boys' yard clear to the Cyclone fence and thought about the hair that I had seen sticking out of the canvas. It was going to be summer soon, so you could feel that freedom coming on too.

I ran back into the girls' yard, and there was the quiet sister all by herself. I ran past her, and she followed me into the girls' lavatory. My footsteps rang hard against cement and tile because of the taps I had nailed into my shoes. Her footsteps were soft, padding after me. There was no one in the lavatory but the two of us. I ran all around the rows of twenty-five open stalls to make sure of that. No sisters. I think we must have been playing hide-and-go-seek. She was not good at hiding by herself and usually followed her sister; they'd hide in the same place. They must have gotten separated. In this growing twilight, a child could hide and never be found.

I stopped abruptly in front of the sinks, and she came running toward me before she could stop herself, so that she almost collided with me. I walked closer. She backed away, puzzlement, then alarm in her eyes.

"You're going to talk," I said, my voice steady and normal, as it is when talking to the familiar, the weak, and the small. "I am going to make you talk, you sissy-girl." She stopped backing away and stood fixed.

I looked into her face so I could hate it close up. She

wore black bangs, and her cheeks were pink and white. She was baby soft. I thought that I could put my thumb on her nose and push it bonelessly in, indent her face. I could poke dimples into her cheeks. I could work her face around like dough. She stood still, and I did not want to look at her face anymore; I hated fragility. I walked around her, looked her up and down the way the Mexican and Negro girls did when they fought, so tough. I hated her weak neck, the way it did not support her head but let it droop; her head would fall backward. I stared at the curve of her nape. I wished I was able to see what my own neck looked like from the back and sides. I hoped it did not look like hers; I wanted a stout neck. I grew my hair long to hide it in case it was a flower-stem neck. I walked around to the front of her to hate her face some more.

I reached up and took the fatty part of her cheek, not dough, but meat, between my thumb and finger. This close, and I saw no pores. "Talk," I said. "Are you going to talk?" Her skin was fleshy, like squid out of which the glassy blades of bones had been pulled. I wanted tough skin, hard brown skin. I had callused my hands; I had scratched dirt to blacken the nails, which I cut straight across to make stubby fingers. I gave her face a squeeze. "Talk." When I let go, the pink rushed back into my white thumbprint on her skin. I walked around to her side. "Talk!" I shouted into the side of her head. Her straight hair hung, the same all these years, no ringlets or braids or permanents. I squeezed her other cheek. "Are you? Huh? Are you going to talk?" She tried to shake her head, but I had hold of her face. She had no muscles to jerk away. Her skin seemed to stretch. I let go in horror. What if it came away in my hand? "No, huh?" I said, rubbing the touch of her off my fingers. "Say 'No,' then," I said. I gave her another pinch and a twist. "Say 'No.'" She shook her head, her straight hair turning with her head, not swinging side to side like the pretty girls'. She was so neat. Her neatness bothered me. I hated the way she folded the wax paper from her lunch; she did not wad her brown paper bag and her school papers. I hated her clothes—the blue pastel cardigan, the white blouse with the collar that lay flat over the cardigan, the homemade flat, cotton skirt she wore when everybody else was wearing flared skirts. I hated pastels; I would wear black always. I squeezed again, harder, even though her cheek had a weak rubbery feeling I did not like. I squeezed one cheek, then the other, back and forth until the tears ran out of her eyes as if I had pulled them out. "Stop crying," I said, but although she habitually followed me around, she did not obey. Her eyes dripped; her nose dripped. She wiped her eyes with her papery fingers. The skin on her hands and arms seemed powdery-dry, like tracing paper, onion skin. I hated her fingers. I could snap them like breadsticks. I pushed her hands down. "Say 'Hi,' " I said. " 'Hi.' Like that. Say your name. Go ahead. Say it. Or are you stupid? You're so stupid, you don't know your own name, is that it? When I say, 'What's your name?' you just blurt it out, o.k.? What's your name?" Last year the whole class had laughed at a boy who couldn't fill out a form because he didn't know his father's name. The teacher sighed, exasperated, and was very sarcastic, "Don't you notice things? What does your mother call him?" she said. The class laughed at how dumb he was not to notice things. "She calls him father of me," he said. Even we laughed, although we knew that his mother did not call his father by name, and a son does not know his father's name. We laughed and were relieved that our parents had had the foresight to tell us some names we could give the teachers. "If you're not stupid," I said to the quiet girl, "what's your name?" She shook her head, and some hair caught in the tears; wet black hair stuck to the side of the pink and white face. I reached up (she was taller than I) and took a strand of hair. I pulled it. "Well, then, let's honk your hair," I said. "Honk. Honk." Then I pulled the other side —"ho-o-n-nk"—a long pull; "ho-o-n-n-nk"—a longer pull. I could see her little white ears, like white cutworms curled underneath the hair. "Talk!" I yelled into each cutworm.

I looked right at her. "I know you talk," I said. "I've

heard you." Her eyebrows flew up. Something in those black eyes was startled, and I pursued it. "I was walking past your house when you didn't know I was there. I heard you yell in English and in Chinese. You weren't just talking. You were shouting. I heard you shout. You were saying, 'Where are you?' Say that again. Go ahead, just the way you did at home." I yanked harder on the hair, but steadily, not jerking. I did not want to pull it out. "Go ahead. Say, 'Where are you?' Say it loud enough for your sister to come. Call her. Make her come help you. Call her name. I'll stop if she comes. So call. Go ahead."

She shook her head, her mouth curved down, crying. I could see her tiny white teeth, baby teeth. I wanted to grow big strong yellow teeth. "You do have a tongue," I said. "So use it." I pulled the hair at her temples, pulled the tears out of her eyes. "Say, 'Ow,'" I said. "Just 'Ow.' Say, 'Let go.' Go ahead. Say it. I'll honk you again if you don't say, 'Let me alone.' Say, 'Leave me alone,' and I'll let you go. I will. I'll let go if you say it. You can stop this anytime you want to, you know. All you have to do is tell me to stop. Just say, 'Stop.' You're just asking for it, aren't you? You're just asking for another honk. Well then, I'll have to give you another honk. Say, 'Stop.'" But she didn't. I had to pull again and again.

Sounds did come out of her mouth, sobs, chokes, noises that were almost words. Snot ran out of her nose. She tried to wipe it on her hands, but there was too much of it. She used her sleeve. "You're disgusting," I told her. "Look at you, snot streaming down your nose, and you won't say a word to stop it. You're such a nothing." I moved behind her and pulled the hair growing out of her weak neck. I let go. I stood silent for a long time. Then I screamed, "Talk!" I would scare the words out of her. If she had had little bound feet, the toes twisted under the balls, I would have jumped up and landed on them—crunch!—stomped on them with my iron shoes. She cried hard, sobbing aloud. "Cry, 'Mama,'" I said. "Come on. Cry, 'Mama.' Say, 'Stop it.'"

I put my finger on her pointed chin. "I don't like you. I don't like the weak little toots you make on your flute. Wheeze. Wheeze. I don't like the way you don't swing at the ball. I don't like the way you're the last one chosen. I don't like the way you can't make a fist for tetherball. Why don't you make a fist? Come on. Get tough. Come on. Throw fists." I pushed at her long hands; they swung limply at her sides. Her fingers were so long, I thought maybe they had an extra joint. They couldn't possibly make fists like other people's. "Make a fist," I said. "Come on. Just fold those fingers up; fingers on the inside, thumbs on the outside. Say something. Honk me back. You're so tall, and you let me pick on you.

"Would you like a hanky? I can't get you one with embroidery on it or crocheting along the edges, but I'll get you some toilet paper if you tell me to. Go ahead. Ask me. I'll get it for you if you ask." She did not stop crying. "Why don't you scream, 'Help'?" I suggested. "Say, 'Help.' Go ahead." She cried on. "O.K. O.K. Don't talk. Just scream, and I'll let you go. Won't that feel good? Go ahead. Like this." I screamed, not too loudly. My voice hit the tile and rang it as if I had thrown a rock at it. The stalls opened wider and the toilets wider and darker. Shadows leaned at angles I had not seen before. It was very late. Maybe a janitor had locked me in with this girl for the night. Her black eyes blinked and stared, blinked and stared. I felt dizzy from hunger. We had been in this lavatory together forever. My mother would call the police again if I didn't bring my sister home soon. "I'll let you go if you say just one word," I said. "You can even say, 'a' or 'the,' and I'll let you go. Come on. Please." She didn't shake her head anymore, only cried steadily, so much water coming out of her. I could see the two duct holes where the tears welled out. Quarts of tears but no words. I grabbed her by the shoulder. I could feel bones. The light was coming in queerly through the frosted glass with the chicken wire embedded in it. Her crying was like an animal's—a seal's

—and it echoed around the basement. "Do you want to stay here all night?" I asked. "Your mother is wondering what happened to her baby. You wouldn't want to have her mad at you. You'd better say something." I shook her shoulder. I pulled her hair again. I squeezed her face. "Come on! Talk! Talk! Talk!" She didn't seem to feel it anymore when I pulled her hair. "There's nobody here but you and me. This isn't a classroom or a playground or a crowd. I'm just one person. You can talk in front of one person. Don't make me pull harder and harder until you talk." But her hair seemed to stretch; she did not say a word. "I'm going to pull harder. Don't make me pull anymore, or your hair will come out and you're going to be bald. Do you want to be bald? You don't want to be bald, do you?"

Far away, coming from the edge of town, I heard whistles blow. The cannery was changing shifts, letting out the afternoon people, and still we were here at school. It was a sad sound—work done. The air was lonelier after the sound died.

"Why won't you talk?" I started to cry. What if I couldn't stop, and everyone would want to know what happened? "Now look what you've done," I scolded. "You're going to pay for this. I want to know why. And you're going to tell me why. You don't see I'm trying to help you out, do you? Do you want to be like this, dumb (do you know what dumb means?), your whole life? Don't you ever want to be a cheerleader? Or a pompon girl? What are you going to do for a living? Yeah, you're going to have to work because you can't be a housewife. Somebody has to marry you before you can be a housewife. And you, you are a plant. Do you know that? That's all you are if you don't talk. If you don't talk, you can't have a personality. You'll have no personality and no hair. You've got to let people know you have a personality and a brain. You think somebody is going to take care of you all your stupid life? You think you'll always have your big sister? You think somebody's going to marry you, is that it? Well, you're not the type that gets dates.

let alone gets married. Nobody's going to notice you. And you have to talk for interviews, speak right up in front of the boss. Don't you know that? You're so dumb. Why do I waste my time on you?" Sniffling and snorting, I couldn't stop crying and talking at the same time. I kept wiping my nose on my arm, my sweater lost somewhere (probably not worn because my mother said to wear a sweater). It seemed as if I had spent my life in that basement, doing the worst thing I had yet done to another person. "I'm doing this for your own good," I said. "Don't you dare tell anyone I've been bad to you. Talk. Please talk."

I was getting dizzy from the air I was gulping. Her sobs and my sobs were bouncing wildly off the tile, sometimes together, sometimes alternating. "I don't understand why you won't say just one word," I cried, clenching my teeth. My knees were shaking, and I hung on to her hair to stand up. Another time I'd stayed too late, I had had to walk around two Negro kids who were bonking each other's head on the concrete. I went back later to see if the concrete had cracks in it. "Look. I'll give you something if you talk. I'll give you my pencil box. I'll buy you some candy. O.K.? What do you want? Tell me. Just say it, and I'll give it to you. Just say, 'yes,' or, 'O.K.,' or, 'Baby Ruth.'" But she didn't want anything.

I had stopped pinching her cheek because I did not like the feel of her skin. I would go crazy if it came away in my hands. "I skinned her," I would have to confess.

Suddenly I heard footsteps hurrying through the basement, and her sister ran into the lavatory calling her name. "Oh, there you are," I said. "We've been waiting for you. I was only trying to teach her to talk. She wouldn't cooperate, though." Her sister went into one of the stalls and got handfuls of toilet paper and wiped her off. Then we found my sister, and we walked home together. "Your family really ought to force her to speak," I advised all the way home. "You mustn't pamper her."

The world is sometimes just, and I spent the next

eighteen months sick in bed with a mysterious illness. There was no pain and no symptoms, though the middle line in my left palm broke in two. Instead of starting junior high school, I lived like the Victorian recluses I read about. I had a rented hospital bed in the living room, where I watched soap operas on t.v., and my family cranked me up and down. I saw no one but my family, who took good care of me. I could have no visitors, no other relatives, no villagers. My bed was against the west window, and I watched the seasons change the peach tree. I had a bell to ring for help. I used a bedpan. It was the best year and a half of my life. Nothing happened.

But one day my mother, the doctor, said, "You're ready to get up today. It's time to get up and go to school." I walked about outside to get my legs working, leaning on a staff I cut from the peach tree. The sky and trees, the sun were immense—no longer framed by a window, no longer grayed with a fly screen. I sat down on the sidewalk in amazement—the night, the stars. But at school I had to figure out again how to talk. I met again the poor girl I had tormented. She had not changed. She wore the same clothes, hair cut, and manner as when we were in elementary school, no make-up on the pink and white face, while the other Asian girls were starting to tape their eyelids. She continued to be able to read aloud. But there was hardly any reading aloud anymore, less and less as we got into high school.

I was wrong about nobody taking care of her. Her sister became a clerk-typist and stayed unmarried. They lived with their mother and father. She did not have to leave the house except to go to the movies. She was supported. She was protected by her family, as they would normally have done in China if they could have afforded it, not sent off to school with strangers, ghosts, boys.

We have so many secrets to hold in. Our sixth grade teacher, who liked to explain things to children, let us read our files. My record shows that I flunked kindergarten and in first grade had no IQ—a zero IQ. I did remember the first grade teacher calling out during a test, while students marked X's on a girl or a boy or a dog, which I covered with black. First grade was when I discovered eye control; with my seeing I could shrink the teacher down to a height of one inch, gesticulating and mouthing on the horizon. I lost this power in sixth grade for lack of practice, the teacher a generous man. "Look at your family's old addresses and think about how you've moved," he said. I looked at my parents' aliases and their birthdays, which variants I knew. But when I saw Father's occupations I exclaimed, "Hey, he wasn't a farmer, he was a . . ." He had been a gambler. My throat cut off the word—silence in front of the most understanding teacher. There were secrets never to be said in front of the ghosts, immigration secrets whose telling could get us sent back to China.

Sometimes I hated the ghosts for not letting us talk; sometimes I hated the secrecy of the Chinese. "Don't tell," said my parents, though we couldn't tell if we wanted to because we didn't know. Are there really secret trials with our own judges and penalties? Are there really flags in Chinatown signaling what stowaways have arrived in San Francisco Bay, their names, and which ships they came on? "Mother, I heard some kids say there are flags like that. Are there? What colors are they? Which buildings do they fly from?"

"No. No, there aren't any flags like that. They're just talking-story. You're always believing talk-story."

"I won't tell anybody, Mother. I promise. Which buildings are the flags on? Who flies them? The benevolent associations?"

"I don't know. Maybe the San Francisco villagers do that; our villagers don't do that."

"What do our villagers do?"

They would not tell us children because we had been born among ghosts, were taught by ghosts, and were ourselves ghost-like. They called us a kind of ghost. Ghosts are noisy and full of air; they talk during meals. They talk about anything.

"Do we send up signal kites? That would be a good idea, huh? We could fly them from the school balcony." Instead of cheaply stringing dragonflies by the tail, we could fly expensive kites, the sky splendid in Chinese colors, distracting ghost eyes while the new people sneak in. Don't tell. "Never tell."

Occasionally the rumor went about that the United States immigration authorities had set up headquarters in the San Francisco or Sacramento Chinatown to urge wetbacks and stowaways, anybody here on fake papers, to come to the city and get their files straightened out. The immigrants discussed whether or not to turn themselves in. "We might as well," somebody would say. "Then we'd have our citizenship for real."

"Don't be a fool," somebody else would say. "It's a trap. You go in there saying you want to straighten out your papers, they'll deport you."

"No, they won't. They're promising that nobody is going to go to jail or get deported. They'll give you citizenship as a reward for turning yourself in, for your honesty."

"Don't you believe it. So-and-so trusted them, and he was deported. They deported his children too."

"Where can they send us now? Hong Kong? Taiwan? I've never been to Hong Kong or Taiwan. The Big Six? Where?" We don't belong anywhere since the Revolution. The old China has disappeared while we've been away.

"Don't tell," advised my parents. "Don't go to San Francisco until they leave."

Lie to Americans. Tell them you were born during the San Francisco earthquake. Tell them your birth certificate and your parents were burned up in the fire. Don't report crimes; tell them we have no crimes and no poverty. Give a new name every time you get arrested; the ghosts won't recognize you. Pay the new immigrants twenty-five cents an hour and say we have no unemployment. And, of course, tell them we're against Communism. Ghosts have no memory anyway and poor eyesight. And the Han people won't be pinned down.

Even the good things are unspeakable, so how could I ask about deformities? From the configurations of food my mother set out, we kids had to infer the holidays. She did not whip us up with holiday anticipation or explain. You only remembered that perhaps a year ago you had eaten monk's food, or that there was meat, and it was a meat holiday; or you had eaten moon cakes or long noodles for long life (which is a pun). In front of the whole chicken with its slit throat toward the ceiling, she'd lay out just so many pairs of chopsticks alternating with wine cups, which were not for us because there were a different number from the number in our family, and they were set too close together for us to sit at. To sit at one of those place settings a being would have to be about two inches wide, a tall wisp of an invisibility. Mother would pour Seagram's 7 into the cups and, after a while, pour it back into the bottle. Never explaining. How can Chinese keep any traditions at all? They don't even make you pay attention, slipping in a ceremony and clearing the table before the children notice specialness. The adults get mad, evasive, and shut you up if you ask. You get no warning that you shouldn't wear a white ribbon in your hair until they hit you and give you the sideways glare for the rest of the day. They hit you if you wave brooms around or drop chopsticks or drum them. They hit you if you wash your hair on certain days, or tap somebody with a ruler, or step over a brother whether it's during your menses or not. You figure out what you got hit for and don't do it again if you figured correctly. But I think that if you don't figure it out, it's all right. Then you can grow up bothered by "neither ghosts nor deities." "Gods you avoid won't hurt you." I don't see how they kept up a continuous culture for five thousand years. Maybe they didn't; maybe everyone makes it up as they go along. If we had to depend on being told, we'd have no religion, no babies, no menstruation (sex, of course, unspeakable), no death.

I thought talking and not talking made the difference between sanity and insanity. Insane people were the ones who couldn't explain themselves. There were many crazy girls and women. Perhaps the sane people stayed in China to build the new, sane society. Or perhaps our little village had become odd in its isolation. No other Chinese, neither the ones in Sacramento, nor the ones in San Francisco, nor Hawaii speak like us. Within a few blocks of our house were half a dozen crazy women and girls, all belonging to village families.

There was the woman next door who was chatty one moment—inviting us children to our first "sky movie"— and shut up the next. Then we would see silver heat rise from her body; it solidified before our eyes. She made us afraid, though she said nothing, did nothing. Her husband threw the loudspeaker out the window and drove home fast in the middle of the show. She sat like stone in the front seat; he had to open the door for her and help her out. She slammed the door. After they went inside, we could hear doors slamming throughout their house. They did not have children, so it was not children slamming doors. The next day, she disappeared, and people would say she had been taken to Napa or Agnew. When a woman disappeared or reappeared after an absence, people whispered, "Napa." "Agnew." She had been locked up before. Her husband rented out the house and also went away. The last time he had left town, he had been single. He had gone back to China, where he had bought her and married her. Now while she was locked up in the asylum, he went, people said, to the Midwest. A year or two passed. He returned to Napa to drive her home. As a present, he had brought with him from the Midwest a child, half Chinese and half white. People said it was his illegitimate son. She was very happy to have a son to raise in her old age, although I saw that the boy hit her to get candy and toys. She was the one who died happy, sitting on the steps after cooking dinner.

There was Crazy Mary, whose family were Christian converts. Her mother and father had come to the Gold

Mountain leaving Mary, a toddler, in China. By the time they made enough money to send for her, having replaced the horse and vegetable wagon with a truck, she was almost twenty and crazy. Her parents often said, "We thought she'd be grown but young enough to learn English and translate for us." Their other children, who were born in the U.S., were normal and could translate. I was glad that I was born nine months after my mother emigrated. Crazy Mary was a large girl and had a big black mole on her face, which is a sign of fortune. The black mole pulls you forward with its power; a mole at the back of the head pulls you back. She seemed cheerful, but pointed at things that were not there. I disliked looking at her; you never knew what you were going to see, what rictus would shape her face. Or what you would hear—growls, laughs. Her head hung like a bull's, and her eyes peeked at you out of her hair. Her face was a white blur because she was indoors so much and also because I tried not to look at her directly. She often had rice on her face and in her hair. Her mother cut her hair neatly around her ears, stubble at the back of her neck. She wore pajamas, a rough brown sweater buttoned crooked, and a big apron, not a work apron but a bib. She wore slippers, and you could see her thick ankles naked, her naked heels and tendons. When you went to her house, you had to keep alert because you didn't want her to come at you from around a corner, her hands loose. She would lurch out of dark corners; houses with crazy girls have locked rooms and drawn curtains. A smell came from her which would not have been unpleasant had it belonged to someone else. The house smelled of her, camphoraceous. Maybe they tied camphor on her pulse to cure her. Our mother used to tie dried prunes stuffed with camphor to our wrists. We got very embarrassed at school when the rags came loose and their contents fell out in clumps and grains. Crazy Mary did not improve, and so she too was locked up in the crazyhouse. She was never released. Her family said she liked it there.

There was a slough where our mother took us to pick

orange berries. We carried them home in pots and bags to cook in an egg soup. It was not a wild slough, although tules, cattails and foxtails still grew, also dill, and yellow chamomile, fat and fuzzy as bees. People had been known to have followed the hobo paths and parted the tall stalks to find dead bodies—hobos, Chinese suicides, children. Red-winged blackbirds, whose shoulders were the same color as the berries, perched on a wood bridge, really a train trestle. When a train heaved across it, the black steam engine swollen to bursting like the boiler at the laundry, the birds flew up like Halloween.

We were not the only people who picked in the slough; a witchwoman also went there. One of my brothers named her Pee-A-Nah, which does not have a meaning. Of all the crazy ladies, she was the one who was the village idiot, the public one. When our mother was with us, she would chase the witchwoman away. We'd stand beside and behind our mother, who would say to her, "Leave us alone now" or "Good morning," and Pee-A-Nah would go away. But when we were by ourselves, she chased us. "Pee-A-Nah!" we'd scream. We'd run, terrified, along the hobo paths, over the trestle, and through the streets. Kids said she was a witch capable of witch deeds, unspeakable boilings and tearings apart and transformations if she caught us. "She'll touch you on the shoulder, and you'll not be you anymore. You'd be a piece of glass winking and blinking to people on the sidewalk." She came riding to the slough with a broom between her legs, and she had powdered one cheek red and one white. Her hair stood up and out to the sides in dry masses, black even though she was old. She wore a pointed hat and layers of capes, shawls, sweaters buttoned at the throat like capes, the sleeves flying behind like sausage skins. She came to the slough not to harvest the useful herbs and berries the way we did, but to collect armfuls of cattails and tall grasses and tuber flowers. Sometimes she carried her broomstick horse like a staff. In the fall (she would be such a sight in the fall) she ran "faster than a swallow,"

her cattails popping seed, white seed puffs blowing after
her, clouds of fairies dancing over her head. She streamed
color and flapped in layers. She was an angry witch, not a
happy one. She was fierce; not a fairy, after all, but a
demon. She did run fast, as fast as a child, although she
was a wrinkled woman, an outburst that jumped at us from
bushes, between cars, between buildings. We children vowed
that we would never run home if she came after one of
us. No matter what she did to us, we had to run in the
opposite direction from home. We didn't want her to know
where we lived. If we couldn't outrun her and lose her, we'd
die alone. Once she spotted my sister in our yard, opened the
gate, and chased her up the stairs. My sister screamed and
cried, banging on the door. Our mother let her in quickly,
looking frightened as she fumbled at the latches to lock out
Pee-A-Nah. My sister had to be chanted out of her screaming. It was a good thing Pee-A-Nah had a short memory
because she did not find our house again. Sometimes when a
bunch of tules and reeds and grasses mixed and blew and
waved, I was terrified that it was she, that she was carrying
them or parting them. One day we realized that we had
not seen her for a while. We forgot her, never seeing her
again. She had probably been locked up in the crazyhouse
too.

I had invented a quill pen out of a peacock feather, but
stopped writing with it when I saw that it waved like a
one-eyed slough plant.

I thought every house had to have its crazy woman or
crazy girl, every village its idiot. Who would be It at our
house? Probably me. My sister did not start talking among
nonfamily until a year after I started, but she was neat
while I was messy, my hair tangled and dusty. My dirty
hands broke things. Also I had had the mysterious illness.
And there were adventurous people inside my head to whom
I talked. With them I was frivolous and violent, orphaned.
I was white and had red hair, and I rode a white horse.
Once when I realized how often I went away to see these

free movies, I asked my sister, just checking to see if hearing voices in motors and seeing cowboy movies on blank walls was normal, I asked, "Uh," trying to be casual, "do you talk to people that aren't real inside your mind?"

"Do I *what?*" she said.

"Never mind," I said fast. "Never mind. Nothing."

My sister, my almost-twin, the person most like me in all the world, had said, "*What?*"

I had vampire nightmares; every night the fangs grew longer, and my angel wings turned pointed and black. I hunted humans down in the long woods and shadowed them with my blackness. Tears dripped from my eyes, but blood dripped from my fangs, blood of the people I was supposed to love.

I did not want to be our crazy one. Quite often the big loud women came shouting into the house, "Now when you sell this one, I'd like to buy her to be my maid." Then they laughed. They always said that about my sister, not me because I dropped dishes at them. I picked my nose while I was cooking and serving. My clothes were wrinkled even though we owned a laundry. Indeed I was getting stranger every day. I affected a limp. And, of course, the mysterious disease I had had might have been dormant and contagious.

But if I made myself unsellable here, my parents need only wait until China, and there, where anything happens, they would be able to unload us, even me—sellable, marriageable. So while the adults wept over the letters about the neighbors gone berserk turning Communist ("They do funny dances; they sing weird songs, just syllables. They make us dance; they make us sing"), I was secretly glad. As long as the aunts kept disappearing and the uncles dying after unspeakable tortures, my parents would prolong their Gold Mountain stay. We could start spending our fare money on a car and chairs, a stereo. Nobody wrote to tell us that Mao himself had been matched to an older girl when he was a child and that he was freeing women from prisons, where they had been put for refusing the businessmen their parents had picked as husbands. Nobody told us that the

Revolution (the Liberation) was against girl slavery and girl infanticide (a village-wide party if it's a boy). Girls would no longer have to kill themselves rather than get married. May the Communists light up the house on a girl's birthday.

I watched our parents buy a sofa, then a rug, curtains, chairs to replace the orange and apple crates one by one, now to be used for storage. Good. At the beginning of the second Communist five-year plan, our parents bought a car. But you could see the relatives and the villagers getting more worried about what to do with the girls. We had three girl second cousins, no boys; their great-grandfather and our grandfather were brothers. The great-grandfather was the old man who lived with them, as the river-pirate great-uncle was the old man who lived with us. When my sisters and I ate at their house, there we would be—six girls eating. The old man opened his eyes wide at us and turned in a circle, surrounded. His neck tendons stretched out. "Maggots!" he shouted. "Maggots! Where are my grandsons? I want grandsons! Give me grandsons! Maggots!" He pointed at each one of us, "Maggot! Maggot! Maggot! Maggot! Maggot! Maggot!" Then he dived into his food, eating fast and getting seconds. "Eat, maggots," he said. "Look at the maggots chew."

"He does that at every meal," the girls told us in English.

"Yeah," we said. "Our old man hates us too. What assholes."

Third Grand-Uncle finally did get a boy, though, his only great-grandson. The boy's parents and the old man bought him toys, bought him everything—new diapers, new plastic pants—not homemade diapers, not bread bags. They gave him a full-month party inviting all the emigrant villagers; they deliberately hadn't given the girls parties, so that no one would notice another girl. Their brother got toy trucks that were big enough to climb inside. When he grew older, he got a bicycle and let the girls play with his old tricycle and wagon. My mother bought his sisters a typewriter.

"They can be clerk-typists," their father kept saying, but he would not buy them a typewriter.

"What an asshole," I said, muttering the way my father muttered "Dog vomit" when the customers nagged him about missing socks.

Maybe my mother was afraid that I'd say things like that out loud and so had cut my tongue. Now again plans were urgently afoot to fix me up, to improve my voice. The wealthiest villager wife came to the laundry one day to have a listen. "You better do something with this one," she told my mother. "She has an ugly voice. She quacks like a pressed duck." Then she looked at me unnecessarily hard; Chinese do not have to address children directly. "You have what we call a pressed-duck voice," she said. This woman was the giver of American names, a powerful namer, though it was American names; my parents gave the Chinese names. And she was right: if you squeezed the duck hung up to dry in the east window, the sound that was my voice would come out of it. She was a woman of such power that all we immigrants and descendants of immigrants were obliged to her family forever for bringing us here and for finding us jobs, and she had named my voice.

"No," I quacked. "No, I don't."

"Don't talk back," my mother scolded. Maybe this lady was powerful enough to send us back.

I went to the front of the laundry and worked so hard that I impolitely did not take notice of her leaving.

"Improve that voice," she had instructed my mother, "or else you'll never marry her off. Even the fool half ghosts won't have her." So I discovered the next plan to get rid of us: marry us off here without waiting until China. The villagers' peasant minds converged on marriage. Late at night when we walked home from the laundry, they should have been sleeping behind locked doors, not overflowing into the streets in front of the benevolent associations, all alit. We stood on tiptoes and on one another's shoulders, and through the door we saw spotlights open on tall singers afire with sequins. An opera from San Francisco! An opera from Hong Kong! Usually I did not understand the words in operas, whether because of our obscure dialect or theirs I didn't know, but I heard one line sung out into the night air in a woman's voice high and clear as ice. She was standing on a chair, and she sang, "Beat me, then, beat me." The crowd laughed until the tears rolled down their cheeks while the cymbals clashed—the dragon's copper laugh—and the drums banged like firecrackers. "She is playing the part of a new daughter-in-law," my mother explained. "Beat me, then, beat me," she sang again and again. It must have been a refrain; each time she sang it, the audience broke up laughing. Men laughed; women laughed. They were having a great time.

"Chinese smeared bad daughters-in-law with honey and tied them naked on top of ant nests," my father said. "A husband may kill a wife who disobeys him. Confucius said that." Confucius, the rational man.

The singer, I thought, sounded like me talking, yet everyone said, "Oh, beautiful. Beautiful," when she sang high.

Walking home, the noisy women shook their old heads and sang a folk song that made them laugh uproariously:

> Marry a rooster, follow a rooster.
> Marry a dog, follow a dog.
> Married to a cudgel, married to a pestle,
> Be faithful to it. Follow it.

I learned that young men were placing ads in the *Gold Mountain News* to find wives when my mother and father started answering them. Suddenly a series of new workers showed up at the laundry; they each worked for a week before they disappeared. They ate with us. They talked Chinese with my parents. They did not talk to us. We were to call them "Elder Brother," although they were not related to us. They were all funny-looking FOB's, Fresh-off-the-Boat's, as the Chinese-American kids at school called the young immigrants. FOB's wear high-riding gray slacks and white shirts with the sleeves rolled up. Their eyes do not focus correctly—shifty-eyed—and they hold their mouths slack, not tight-jawed masculine. They shave off their sideburns. The girls said *they'd* never date an FOB. My mother took one home from the laundry, and I saw him looking over our photographs. "This one," he said, picking up my sister's picture.

"No. No," said my mother. "This one," my picture. "The oldest first," she said. Good. I was an obstacle. I would protect my sister and myself at the same time. As my parents and the FOB sat talking at the kitchen table, I dropped two dishes. I found my walking stick and limped across the floor. I twisted my mouth and caught my hand in the knots of my hair. I spilled soup on the FOB when I handed him his bowl. "She can sew, though," I heard my mother say, "and sweep." I raised dust swirls sweeping around and under the FOB's chair—very bad luck because spirits live inside the broom. I put on my shoes with the open flaps and flapped about like a Wino Ghost. From then on, I wore those shoes to parties, whenever the mothers gathered to talk about marriages. The FOB and my parents paid me no attention, half ghosts half invisible, but when he left, my mother yelled at me about the dried-duck voice, the bad temper, the laziness, the clumsiness, the stupidity that comes from reading too much. The young men stopped visiting; not one came back. "Couldn't you just stop rubbing your nose?" she scolded. "All the village ladies are talking about your nose. They're afraid to eat our pastries because you might have kneaded the dough." But I couldn't stop at will anymore, and a crease developed across the bridge. My parents would not give up, though. "Though you can't see it," my mother said, "a red string around your ankle ties you to the person you'll marry. He's already been born, and he's on the other end of the string."

At Chinese school there was a mentally retarded boy who followed me around, probably believing that we were two of a kind. He had an enormous face, and he growled.

He laughed from so far within his thick body that his face got confused about what the sounds coming up into his mouth might be, laughs or cries. He barked unhappily. He didn't go to classes but hung around the playgrounds. We suspected he was not a boy but an adult. He wore baggy khaki trousers like a man's. He carried bags of toys for giving to certain children. Whatever you wanted, he'd get it for you—brand-new toys, as many as you could think up in your poverty, all the toys you never had when you were younger. We wrote lists, discussed our lists, compared them. Those kids not in his favor gave lists to those who were. "Where do you get the toys?" I asked. "I . . . own . . . stores," he roared, one word at a time, thick tongued. At recess the day after ordering, we got handed out to us coloring books, paint sets, model kits. But sometimes he chased us—his fat arms out to the side; his fat fingers opening and closing; his legs stiff like Frankenstein's monster, like the mummy dragging its foot; growling; laughing-crying. Then we'd have to run, following the old rule, running away from our house.

But suddenly he knew where we worked. He found us; maybe he had followed us in his wanderings. He started sitting at our laundry. Many of the storekeepers invited sitting in their stores, but we did not have sitting because the laundry was hot and because it was outside Chinatown. He sweated; he panted, the stubble rising and falling on his fat neck and chin. He sat on two large cartons that he brought with him and stacked one on top of the other. He said hello to my mother and father, and then, balancing his heavy head, he lowered himself carefully onto his cartons and sat. My parents allowed this. They did not chase him out or comment about how strange he was. I stopped placing orders for toys. I didn't limp anymore; my parents would only figure that this zombie and I were a match.

I studied hard, got straight A's, but nobody seemed to see that I was smart and had nothing in common with this monster, this birth defect. At school there were dating and dances, but not for good Chinese girls. "You ought to develop yourself socially as well as mentally," the American teachers, who took me aside, said.

I told nobody about the monster. And nobody else was talking either; no mention about the laundry workers who appeared and disappeared; no mention about the sitter. Maybe I was making it all up, and queer marriage notions did not occur to other people. I had better not say a word, then. Don't give them ideas. Keep quiet.

I pressed clothes—baskets of giants' BVD's, long underwear even in summertime, T-shirts, sweat shirts. Laundry work is men's clothes, unmarried-men's clothes. My back felt sick because it was toward the monster who gave away toys. His lumpishness was sending out germs that would lower my IQ. His leechiness was drawing IQ points out of the back of my head. I maneuvered my work shifts so that my brothers would work the afternoons, when he usually came lumbering into the laundry, but he caught on and began coming during the evening, the cool shift. Then I would switch back to the afternoon or to the early mornings on weekends and in summer, dodging him. I kept my sister with me, protecting her without telling her why. If she hadn't noticed, then I mustn't scare her. "Let's clean house this morning," I'd say. Our other sister was a baby, and the brothers were not in danger. But the were-person would stalk down our street; his thick face smiled between the lettering on the laundry window, and when he saw me working, he shouldered inside. At night I thought I heard his feet dragging around the house, scraping gravel. I sat up to listen to our watchdog prowl the yard, pulling her long chain after her, and that worried me too. I had to do something about that chain, the weight of it scraping her neck fur short. And if she was walking about, why wasn't she barking? Maybe somebody was out there taming her with raw meat. I could not ask for help.

Every day the hulk took one drink from the watercooler and went once to the bathroom, stumbling between the presses into the back of the laundry, big shoes clumping. Then my parents would talk about what could be inside his boxes. Were they filled with toys? With money? When the toilet flushed, they stopped talking about it. But one day he either stayed in the bathroom for a long time or went for a walk and left the boxes unguarded. "Let's open them up," said my mother, and she did. I looked over her shoulder. The two cartons were stuffed with pornography— naked magazines, nudie postcards and photographs.

You would think she'd have thrown him out right then, but my mother said, "My goodness, he's not too stupid to want to find out about women." I heard the old women talk about how he was stupid but very rich.

Maybe because I was the one with the tongue cut loose, I had grown inside me a list of over two hundred things that I had to tell my mother so that she would know the true things about me and to stop the pain in my throat. When I first started counting, I had had only thirty-six items: how I had prayed for a white horse of my own— white, the bad, mournful color—and prayer bringing me to the attention of the god of the black-and-white nuns who gave us "holy cards" in the park. How I wanted the horse to start the movies in my mind coming true. How I had picked on a girl and made her cry. How I had stolen from the cash register and bought candy for everybody I knew, not just brothers and sisters, but strangers too and ghost children. How it was me who pulled up the onions in the garden out of anger. How I had jumped head-first off the dresser, not accidentally, but so I could fly. Then there were my fights at Chinese school. And the nuns who kept stopping us in the park, which was across the street from Chinese school, to tell us that if we didn't get baptized we'd go to a hell like one of the nine Taoist hells forever. And the obscene caller that phoned us at home when the adults were at the laundry. And the Mexican and Filipino girls at school who went to "confession," and how I envied them their white dresses and their chance each Saturday to tell even thoughts that were sinful. If only I could let my mother know the list, she—and the world—would become more like me, and I would never be alone again. I would pick a time of day when my mother was alone and tell her one item a day; I'd be finished in less than a year. If the telling got excruciating and her anger too bad, I'd tell five items once a week like the Catholic girls, and I'd still be through in a year, maybe ten months. My mother's most peaceful time was in the evenings when she starched the white shirts. The laundry would be clean, the gray wood floors sprinkled and swept with water and wet sawdust. She would be wringing shirts at the starch tub and not running about. My father and sisters and brothers would be at their own jobs mending, folding, packaging. Steam would be rising from the starch, the air cool at last. Yes, that would be the time and place for the telling.

And I wanted to ask again why the women in our family have a split nail on our left little toe. Whenever we asked our parents about it, they would glance at each other, embarrassed. I think I've heard one of them say, "She didn't get away." I made up that we are descended from an ancestress who stubbed her toe and fell when running from a rapist. I wanted to ask my mother if I had guessed right.

I hunkered down between the wall and the wicker basket of shirts. I had decided to start with the earliest item—when I had smashed a spider against the white side of the house: it was the first thing I killed. I said, clearly, "I killed a spider," and it was nothing; she did not hit me or throw hot starch at me. It sounded like nothing to me too. How strange when I had had such feelings of death shoot through my hand and into my body so that I would surely die. So I had to continue, of course, and let her know how important it had been. "I returned every day to look at its smear on the side of the house," I said. "It was our old house, the one we lived in until I was five. I went to the wall every day to look. I studied the stain." Relieved because she said nothing but only continued squeezing the starch, I went away feeling pretty good. Just two hundred and six more items to go. I moved carefully all the next day so as not to do anything or have anything happen to me that would make me go back to two hundred and seven again. I'd tell a couple of easy ones and work up to how I had pulled the quiet girl's hair and how I had enjoyed the year being sick. If it was going to be this easy, maybe I could blurt out several a day, maybe an easy one and a hard one. I could go chronologically, or I could work from easy to hard or hard to easy, depending on my mood. On the second night I talked about how I had hinted to a ghost girl that I wished I had a doll of my own until she gave me a head and body to glue together—that she hadn't given it to me of her own generosity but because I had hinted. But on the fifth night (I skipped two to reward myself) I decided it was time to do a really hard one and tell her about the white horse. And suddenly the duck voice came out, which I did not use with the family. "What's it called, Mother"—the duck voice coming out talking to my own mother—"when a person whispers to the head of the sages —no, not the sages, more like the buddhas but not real people like the buddhas (they've always lived in the sky and never turned into people like the buddhas)—and you whisper to them, the boss of them, and ask for things? They're like magicians? What do you call it when you talk to the boss magician?"

" 'Talking-to-the-top-magician,' I guess."

"I did that. Yes. That's it. That's what I did. I talked-to-the-top-magician and asked for a white horse." There. Said.

"Mm," she said, squeezing the starch out of the collar and cuffs. But I had talked, and she acted as if she hadn't heard.

Perhaps she hadn't understood. I had to be more explicit. I hated this. "I kneeled on the bed in there, in the laundry bedroom, and put my arms up like I saw in a comic book"—one night I heard monsters coming through the kitchen, and I had promised the god in the movies, the one the Mexicans and Filipinos have, as in "God Bless America," that I would not read comic books anymore if he would save me just this once; I had broken that promise, and I needed to tell all this to my mother too—"and in that ludicrous position asked for a horse."

"Mm," she said, nodded, and kept dipping and squeezing.

On my two nights off, I had sat on the floor too but had not said a word.

"Mother," I whispered and quacked.

"I can't stand this whispering," she said looking right at me, stopping her squeezing. "Senseless gabbings every night. I wish you would stop. Go away and work. Whispering, whispering, making no sense. Madness. I don't feel like hearing your craziness."

So I had to stop, relieved in some ways. I shut my mouth, but I felt something alive tearing at my throat, bite by bite, from the inside. Soon there would be three hundred things, and too late to get them out before my mother grew old and died.

I had probably interrupted her in the middle of her own quiet time when the boiler and presses were off and the cool night flew against the windows in moths and crickets. Very few customers came in. Starching the shirts for the next day's pressing was probably my mother's time to ride off with the people in her own mind. That would explain why she was so far away and did not want to listen to me. "Leave me alone," she said.

The hulk, the hunching sitter, brought a third box now, to rest his feet on. He patted his boxes. He sat in wait, hunching on his pile of dirt. My throat hurt constantly, vocal cords taut to snapping. One night when the laundry was so busy that the whole family was eating dinner there, crowded around the little round table, my throat burst open. I stood up, talking and burbling. I looked directly at my mother and at my father and screamed, "I want you to tell that hulk, that gorilla-ape, to go away and never bother us again. I know what you're up to. You're thinking he's rich, and we're poor. You think we're odd and not pretty and we're not bright. You think you can give us away to freaks. You better not do that, Mother. I don't want to see him or his dirty boxes here tomorrow. If I see him here one more time, I'm going away. I'm going away anyway. I am. Do you hear me? I may be ugly and clumsy, but one thing I'm not, I'm not retarded. There's nothing wrong with my brain. Do you know what the Teacher Ghosts say about me? They tell me I'm smart, and I can win scholarships. I can get into colleges. I've already applied. I'm smart. I can do all kinds of things. I know how to get A's, and they say I could be a scientist or a mathematician if I want. I can make a living and take care of myself. So you don't have to find me a keeper who's too dumb to know a bad bargain. I'm so smart, if they say write ten pages, I can write fifteen. I can do ghost things even better than ghosts can. Not everybody thinks I'm nothing. I am not going to be a slave or a wife. Even if I am stupid and talk funny and get sick, I won't let you turn me into a slave or a wife. I'm getting out of here. I can't stand living here anymore. It's your fault I talk weird. The only reason I flunked kindergarten was because you couldn't teach me English, and you gave me a zero IQ. I've brought my IQ up, though. They say I'm smart now. Things follow in lines at school. They take stories and teach us to turn them into essays. I don't need anybody to pronounce English words for me. I can figure them out by myself. I'm going to get scholarships, and I'm going away. And at college I'll have the people I like for friends. I don't care if their great-great-grandfather died of TB. I don't care if they were our enemies in China four thousand years ago. So get that ape out of here. I'm going to college. And I'm not going to Chinese school anymore. I'm going to run for office at American school, and I'm going to join clubs. I'm going to get enough offices and clubs on my record to get into college. And I can't stand Chinese school anyway; the kids are rowdy and mean, fighting all night. And I don't want to listen to any more of your stories; they have no logic. They scramble me up. You lie with stories. You won't tell me a story and then say, 'This is a true story,' or, 'This is just a story.' I can't tell the difference. I don't even know what your real names are. I can't tell what's real and what you make up. Ha! You can't stop me from talking. You tried to cut off my tongue, but it didn't work." So I told the hardest ten or twelve things on my list all in one outburst.

My mother, who is champion talker, was, of course, shouting at the same time. "I cut it to make you talk more, not less, you dummy. You're still stupid. You can't listen right. I didn't say I was going to marry you off. Did I ever say that? Did I ever mention that? Those newspaper people were for your sister, not you. Who would want you? Who said we could sell you? We can't sell people. Can't you take a joke? You can't even tell a joke from real life. You're not so smart. Can't even tell real from false."

"I'm never getting married, never!"

"Who'd want to marry you anyway? Noisy. Talking like a duck. Disobedient. Messy. And I know about college. What makes you think you're the first one to think about college? I was a doctor. I went to medical school. I don't see why you have to be a mathematician. I don't see why you can't be a doctor like me."

"I can't stand fever and delirium or listening to people coming out of anesthesia. But I didn't say I wanted to be a mathematician either. That's what the ghosts say. I want to be a lumberjack and a newspaper reporter." Might as well tell her some of the other items on my list. "I'm going to chop down trees in the daytime and write about timber at night."

"I don't see why you need to go to college at all to become either one of those things. Everybody else is sending their girls to typing school. 'Learn to type if you want to be an American girl.' Why don't you go to typing school? The cousins and village girls are going to typing school."

"And you leave my sister alone. You try that with the advertising again, and I'll take her with me." My telling list was scrambled out of order. When I said them out loud I saw that some of the items were ten years old already, and I had outgrown them. But they kept pouring out anyway in the voice like Chinese opera. I could hear the drums and the cymbals and the gongs and brass horns.

"You're the one to leave your little sisters alone," my mother was saying. "You're always leading them off somewhere. I've had to call the police twice because of you." She herself was shouting out things I had meant to tell her— that I took my brothers and sisters to explore strange people's houses, ghost children's houses, and haunted houses blackened by fire. We explored a Mexican house and a redheaded family's house, but not the gypsies' house; I had only seen the inside of the gypsies' house in mind-movies. We explored the sloughs, where we found hobo nests. My mother must have followed us.

"You turned out so unusual. I fixed your tongue so you could say charming things. You don't even say hello to the villagers."

"They don't say hello to me."

"They don't have to answer children. When you get old, people will say hello to you."

"When I get to college, it won't matter if I'm not charming. And it doesn't matter if a person is ugly; she can still do schoolwork."

"I didn't say you were ugly."

"You say that all the time."

"That's what we're supposed to say. That's what Chinese say. We like to say the opposite."

It seemed to hurt her to tell me that—another guilt for

my list to tell my mother, I thought. And suddenly I got very confused and lonely because I was at that moment telling her my list, and in the telling, it grew. No higher listener. No listener but myself.

"Ho Chi Kuei," she shouted. "Ho Chi Kuei. Leave then. Get out, you Ho Chi Kuei. Get out. I knew you were going to turn out bad. Ho Chi Kuei." My brothers and sisters had left the table, and my father would not look at me anymore, ignoring me.

Be careful what you say. It comes true. It comes true. I had to leave home in order to see the world logically, logic the new way of seeing. I learned to think that mysteries are for explanation. I enjoy the simplicity. Concrete pours out of my mouth to cover the forests with freeways and sidewalks. Give me plastics, periodical tables, t.v. dinners with vegetables no more complex than peas mixed with diced carrots. Shine floodlights into dark corners: no ghosts.

I've been looking up "Ho Chi Kuei," which is what the immigrants call us—Ho Chi Ghosts. "Well, Ho Chi Kuei," they say, "what silliness have you been up to now?" "That's a Ho Chi Kuei for you," they say, no matter what we've done. It was more complicated (and therefore worse) than "dog," which they say affectionately, mostly to boys. They use "pig" and "stink pig" for girls, and only in an angry voice. The river-pirate great-uncle called even my middle brother Ho Chi Kuei, and he seemed to like him best. The maggot third great-uncle even shouted "Ho Chi Kuei!" at the boy. I don't know any Chinese I can ask without getting myself scolded or teased, so I've been looking in books. So far I have the following translations for *ho* and/or *chi:* "centipede," "grub," "bastard carp," "chirping insect," "jujube tree," "pied wagtail," "grain sieve," "casket sacrifice," "water lily," "good frying," "non-eater," "dustpan-and-broom" (but that's a synonym for "wife"). Or perhaps I've romanized the spelling wrong and it is *Hao* Chi Kuei, which could mean they are calling us "Good Foundation Ghosts." The immigrants could be saying that we were born on Gold

Mountain and have advantages. Sometimes they scorn us for having had it so easy, and sometimes they're delighted. They also call us "Jook Sing," or "Bamboo Nodes." Bamboo nodes obstruct water.

I like to look up a troublesome, shameful thing and then say, "Oh, is that all?" The simple explanation makes it less scary to go home after yelling at your mother and father. It drives the fear away and makes it possible someday to visit China, where I know now they don't sell girls or kill each other for no reason.

Now colors are gentler and fewer; smells are antiseptic. Now when I peek in the basement window where the villagers say they see a girl dancing like a bottle imp, I can no longer see a spirit in a skirt made of light, but a voiceless girl dancing when she thought no one was looking. The very next day after I talked out the retarded man, the huncher, he disappeared. I never saw him again or heard what became of him. Perhaps I made him up, and what I once had was not Chinese-sight at all but child-sight that would have disappeared eventually without such struggle. The throat pain always returns, though, unless I tell what I really think, whether or not I lose my job, or spit out gaucheries all over a party. I've stopped checking "bilingual" on job applications. I could not understand any of the dialects the interviewer at China Airlines tried on me, and he didn't understand me either. I'd like to go to New Society Village someday and find out exactly how far I can walk before people stop talking like me. I continue to sort out what's just my childhood, just my imagination, just my family, just the village, just movies, just living.

Soon I want to go to China and find out who's lying— the Communists who say they have food and jobs for everybody or the relatives who write that they have not the money to buy salt. My mother sends money she earns working in the tomato fields to Hong Kong. The relatives there can send it on to the remaining aunts and their children and, after a good harvest, to the children and grandchildren of my grandfather's two minor wives. "Every woman in the tomato row is sending money home," my mother says, "to Chinese villages and Mexican villages and Filipino villages and, now, Vietnamese villages, where they speak Chinese too. The women come to work whether sick or well. 'I can't die,' they say, 'I'm supporting fifty,' or 'I'm supporting a hundred.' "

What I'll inherit someday is a green address book full of names. I'll send the relatives money, and they'll write me stories about their hunger. My mother has been tearing up the letters from the youngest grandson of her father's third wife. He has been asking for fifty dollars to buy a bicycle. He says a bicycle will change his life. He could feed his wife and children if he had a bicycle. "We'd have to go hungry ourselves," my mother says. "They don't understand that we have ourselves to feed too." I've been making money; I guess it's my turn. I'd like to go to China and see those people and find out what's a cheat story and what's not. Did my grandmother really live to be ninety-nine? Or did they string us along all those years to get our money? Do the babies wear a Mao button like a drop of blood on their jumpsuits? When we overseas Chinese send money, do the relatives divide it evenly among the commune? Or do they really pay 2 percent tax and keep the rest? It would be good if the Communists were taking care of themselves; then I could buy a color t.v.

Here is a story my mother told me, not when I was young, but recently, when I told her I also talk story. The beginning is hers, the ending, mine.

In China my grandmother loved the theater (which I would not have been able to understand because of my seventh-grade vocabulary, said my mother). When the actors came to the village and set up their scaffolding, my grandmother bought a large section up front. She bought enough room for our entire family and a bed; she would stay days and nights, not missing even the repeating scenes.

The danger was that the bandits would make raids on households thinned out during performances. Bandits followed the actors.

"But, Grandmother," the family complained, "the bandits will steal the tables while we're gone." They took the chairs to plays.

"I want every last one of you at that theater," my grandmother raved. "Slavegirls, everybody. I don't want to watch that play by myself. How can I laugh all by myself? You want me to clap alone, is that it? I want everybody there. Babies, everybody."

"The robbers will ransack the food."

"So let them. Cook up the food and take it to the theater. If you're so worried about bandits, if you're not going to concentrate on the play because of a few bandits, leave the doors open. Leave the windows open. Leave the house wide open. I order the doors open. We are going to the theater without worries."

So they left the doors open, and my whole family went to watch the actors. And sure enough, that night the bandits struck—not the house, but the theater itself. "Bandits aa!" the audience screamed. "Bandits aa!" the actors screamed. My family ran in all directions, my grandmother and mother holding on to each other and jumping into a ditch. They crouched there because my grandmother could run no farther on bound feet. They watched a bandit loop a rope around my youngest aunt, Lovely Orchid, and prepare to drag her off. Suddenly he let her go. "A prettier one," he said, grabbing somebody else. By daybreak, when my grandmother and mother made their way home, the entire family was home safe, proof to my grandmother that our family was immune to harm as long as they went to plays. They went to many plays after that.

I like to think that at some of those performances, they heard the songs of Ts'ai Yen, a poetess born in A.D. 175. She was the daughter of Ts'ai Yung, the scholar famous for his library. When she was twenty years old, she was captured by a chieftain during a raid by the Southern

Hsiung-nu. He made her sit behind him when the tribe rode like the haunted from one oasis to the next, and she had to put her arms around his waist to keep from falling off the horse. After she became pregnant, he captured a mare as his gift to her. Like other captive soldiers until the time of Mao, whose soldiers volunteered, Ts'ai Yen fought desultorily when the fighting was at a distance, and she cut down anyone in her path during the madness of close combat. The tribe fought from horseback, charging in a mass into villages and encampments. She gave birth on the sand; the barbarian women were said to be able to birth in the saddle. During her twelve-year stay with the barbarians, she had two children. Her children did not speak Chinese. She spoke it to them when their father was out of the tent, but they imitated her with senseless singsong words and laughed.

The barbarians were primitives. They gathered inedible reeds when they camped along rivers and dried them in the sun. They dried the reeds tied on their flagpoles and horses' manes and tails. Then they cut wedges and holes. They slipped feathers and arrow shafts into the shorter reeds, which became nock-whistles. During battle the arrows whistled, high whirling whistles that suddenly stopped when the arrows hit true. Even when the barbarians missed, they terrified their enemies by filling the air with death sounds, which Ts'ai Yen had thought was their only music, until one night she heard music tremble and rise like desert wind. She walked out of her tent and saw hundreds of the barbarians sitting upon the sand, the sand gold under the moon. Their elbows were raised, and they were blowing on flutes. They reached again and again for a high note, yearning toward a high note, which they found at last and held—an icicle in the desert. The music disturbed Ts'ai Yen; its sharpness and its cold made her ache. It disturbed her so that she could not concentrate on her own thoughts. Night after night the songs filled the desert no matter how many dunes away she walked. She hid in her tent but could not sleep through the sound. Then, out of Ts'ai Yen's tent, which was apart from the others, the barbarians heard a woman's voice singing, as if to her babies, a song so high and clear, it matched the flutes. Ts'ai Yen sang about China and her family there. Her words seemed to be Chinese, but the barbarians understood their sadness and anger. Sometimes they thought they could catch barbarian phrases about forever wandering. Her children did not laugh, but eventually sang along when she left her tent to sit by the winter campfires, ringed by barbarians.

After twelve years among the Southern Hsiung-nu, Ts'ai Yen was ransomed and married to Tung Ssu so that her father would have Han descendants. She brought her songs back from the savage lands, and one of the three that has been passed down to us is "Eighteen Stanzas for a Barbarian Reed Pipe," a song that Chinese sing to their own instruments. It translated well.

ABOUT THE AUTHOR

Maxine Hong Kingston lives in California with her
husband, actor Earll Kingston. She is also the author
of *China Men* and *Tripmaster Monkey*, which are
available in Vintage International.

TALKING IT OVER
by Julian Barnes

Through the indelible voices of three narrators—two best friends and the woman they both love—Julian Barnes reconstructs the romantic triangle as a weapon whose edges cut like razor blades.

"An interplay of serious thought and dazzling wit.... It's moving, it's funny, it's frightening...fiction at its best."
—*The New York Times Book Review*

Fiction/Literature/0-679-73687-5

. . . .

POSSESSION
by A. S. Byatt

An intellectual mystery and a triumphant love story of a pair of young scholars researching the lives of two Victorian poets.

"Gorgeously written...dazzling...a tour de force."
—*The New York Times Book Review*

Fiction/Literature/0-679-73590-9

. . . .

THE STRANGER
by Albert Camus

Through the story of an ordinary man who unwittingly gets drawn into a senseless murder, Camus explores what he termed "the nakedness of man faced with the absurd."

Fiction/Literature/0-679-72020-0

. . . .

BREAKFAST AT TIFFANY'S
AND THREE STORIES
by Truman Capote

Truman Capote created in Holly Golightly a heroine whose name has entered the American idiom and whose style is now part of the literary landscape. Holly knows that nothing bad can ever happen to you at Tiffany's; her poignancy, wit, and naïveté continue to charm.

Also included in this volume are the stories "House of Flowers," "A Diamond Guitar," and "A Christmas Memory."

"Truman Capote is the most perfect writer of my generation. He writes the best sentences word for word, rhythm upon rhythm." —Norman Mailer

Fiction/Literature/0-679-74565-3

INVISIBLE MAN
by Ralph Ellison

This searing record of a black man's journey through contemporary America reveals, in Ralph Ellison's words, "the sheer rhetorical challenge involved in communicating across our barriers of race and religion, class, color and region."

"The greatest American novel in the second half of the twentieth century...the classic representation of American black experience."   —R.W. B. Lewis

Fiction/Literature/0-679-72313-7

THE SOUND AND THE FURY
by William Faulkner

The tragedy of the Compson family, featuring some of the most memorable characters in American literature: beautiful, rebellious Caddy; the manchild Benjy; haunted, neurotic Quentin; Jason, the brutal cynic; and Dilsey, their black servant.

"For range of effect, philosophical weight, originality of style, variety of characterization, humor, and tragic intensity, [Faulkner's works] are without equal in our time and country."   —Robert Penn Warren

Fiction/Literature/0-679-73224-1

A ROOM WITH A VIEW
by E. M. Forster

Caught up in a world of social snobbery, Lucy Honeychurch breaks from the claustrophobic constraints of her British guardians and takes control of her own fate, finding love with a man whose free spirit reminds her of a "room with a view."

Fiction/Literature/0-679-72476-1

THE REMAINS OF THE DAY
by Kazuo Ishiguro

A profoundly compelling portrait of the perfect English butler and of his fading insular world in postwar England.

"One of the best books of the year."   —The New York Times Book Review

Fiction/Literature/0-679-73172-5/$11.00

THE WOMAN WARRIOR
by Maxine Hong Kingston

"A remarkable book...As an account of growing up female and Chinese American in California, in a laundry of course, it is anti-nostalgic; it burns the fat right out of the mind. As a dream—of the 'female avenger'—it is dizzying, elemental, a poem turned into a sword."   —The New York Times

Nonfiction/Literature/0-679-72188-6

ALL THE PRETTY HORSES
by Cormac McCarthy

At sixteen, John Grady Cole finds himself at the end of a long line of Texas ranchers, cut off from the only life he has ever imagined for himself. With two companions, he sets off for Mexico on a sometimes idyllic, sometimes comic journey, to a place where dreams are paid for in blood.

"A book of remarkable beauty and strength, the work of a master in perfect command of his medium." —*Washington Post Book World*

Winner of the National Book Award for Fiction
Fiction/Literature/0-679-74439-8

. . . .

DEATH IN VENICE
AND SEVEN OTHER STORIES
by Thomas Mann

In addition to "Death in Venice" ("A story," Mann said, "of death...of the voluptuousness of doom"), this volume includes "Mario the Magician," "Disorder and Early Sorrow," "A Man and His Dog," "Felix Krull," "The Blood of the Walsungs," "Tristan," and "Tonio Kröger."

Fiction/Literature/0-679-72206-8

. . . .

LOLITA
by Vladimir Nabokov

The famous and controversial novel that tells the story of the aging Humbert Humbert's obsessive, devouring, and doomed passion for the nymphet Dolores Haze.

"The only convincing love story of our century." —*Vanity Fair*

Fiction/Literature/0-679-72316-1

. . . .

THE ENGLISH PATIENT
by Michael Ondaatje

During the final moments of World War II, four damaged people come together in a deserted Italian villa. As their stories unfold, a complex tapestry of image and emotion, recollection and observation is woven, leaving them inextricably connected by the brutal, improbable circumstances of war.

"It seduces and beguiles us with its many-layered mysteries, its brilliantly taut and lyrical prose, its tender regard for its characters." —*Newsday*

Winner of the Booker Prize
Fiction/Literature/0-679-74520-3

. . . .

MATING
by Norman Rush

A female American anthropologist of high intellect and grand passion, at loose ends in Botswana, finds love with Nelson Denoon, a charismatic intellectual who is rumored to have founded a utopian society in the Kalahari Desert.

"A complex and moving love story...breathtaking in its cunningly intertwined intellectual sweep and brio...a major novel." —*Chicago Tribune*

Winner of the National Book Award for Fiction
Fiction/Literature/0-679-73709-X

....

SOPHIE'S CHOICE
by William Styron

A young Southerner who yearns to become a writer befriends Nathan, a tortured, brilliant Jew, and his beautiful lover, Sophie, becoming a witness to their turbulent love-hate affair and to the burdens of Sophie's unbearable secret.

"Styron's most impressive performance.... It belongs on that small shelf reserved for American masterpieces." —*Washington Post Book World*

Fiction/Literature/0-679-73637-9

....

WATERLAND
by Graham Swift

Set in the bleak Fen country of East Anglia and spanning some 240 years, *Waterland* is "a gothic family saga, a detective story and a philosophical meditation on the nature and uses of history" (*The New York Times*).

"Teems with energy, fertility, violence, madness...demonstrates the irrepressible, wide-ranging talent of this young British writer."

—*Washington Post Book World*

Fiction/Literature/0-679-73979-3

....

THE PASSION
by Jeanette Winterson

Intertwining the destinies of two remarkable people—the soldier Henri, for eight years Napoleon's faithful cook, and Villanelle, the red-haired daughter of a Venetian boatman—*The Passion* is "a deeply imagined and beautiful book, often arrestingly so" (*The New York Times Book Review*).

Fiction/Literature/0-679-72437-0

....

Available at your local bookstore, or call toll-free to order:
1-800-733-3000 (credit cards only).